THE CHEF NEXT DOOR

THE CHEF NEXT DOOR

a pro chef's recipes for fun, fearless home cooking

AMANDA FREITAG

with CARRIE KING

WILLIAM MORROW
An Imprint of HarperCollins*Publishers*

HarperCollins books may be purchased for educational, business, or sales promotional use. For information please e-mail the Special Markets Department at SPsales@harpercollins.com.

FIRST EDITION

Designed by Lorie Pagnozzi
Photography by David Malosh
Food styling by Barrett Washburne

Library of Congress Cataloging-in-Publication Data has been applied for.

ISBN 978-0-06-234583-7

15 16 17 18 19 OV/QGT 10 9 8 7 6 5 4 3 2 1

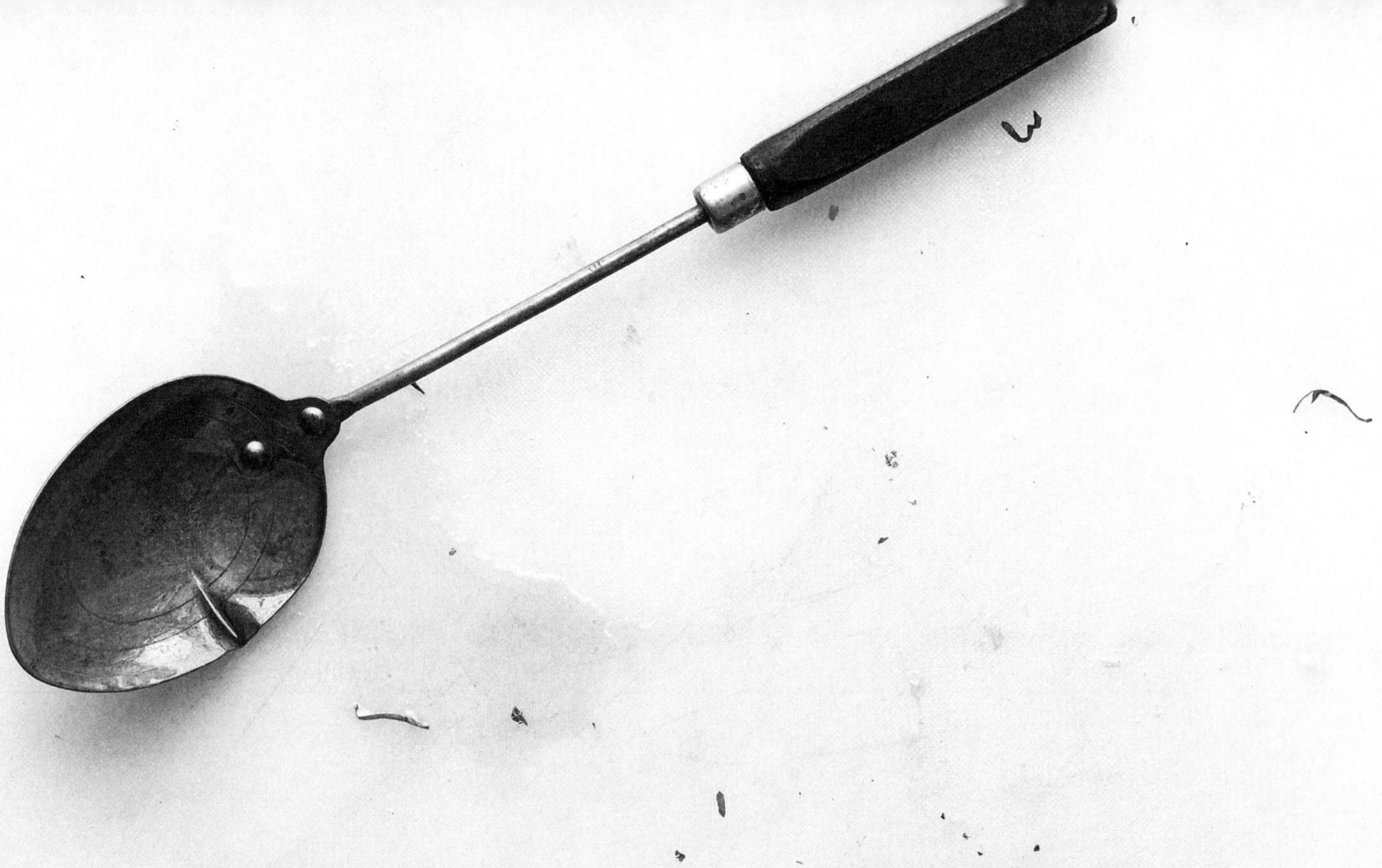

To Pop—I took your advice. When I said I was scared, you said, "What are you worried about? You know what you're doing, just have fun with it." I miss you every second of every day.

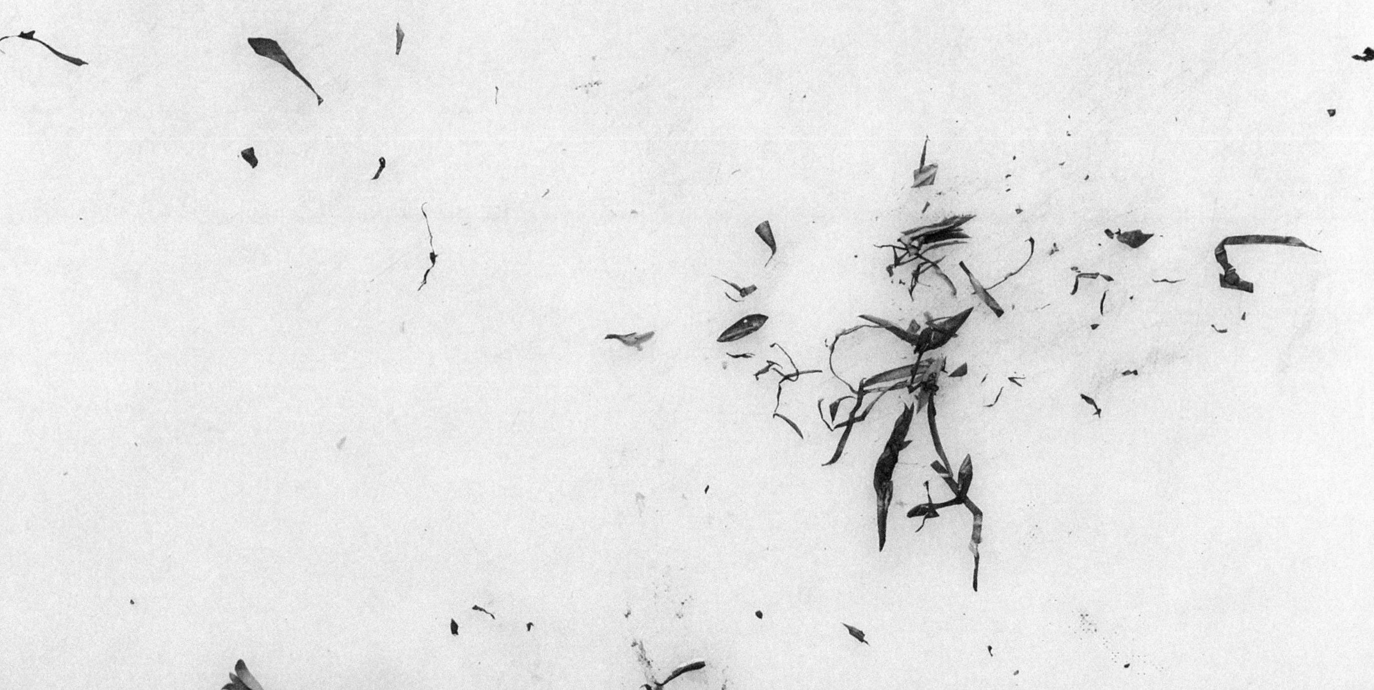

Oven

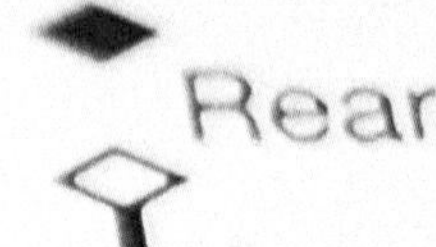
Rear

250 300
OFF

OFF

CONTENTS

INTRODUCTION

When I stand in my kitchen at the Empire Diner, I'm surrounded by frenzied line cooks and servers at the pass frantically looking for orders. I'm enveloped by the unforgiving heat of an arsenal of burners, grills, and convection ovens, all fired up at once. My ears are besieged by the distinct kitchen noise—the dishwasher's constant whir, empty glasses clanking, silverware and plates rattling onto trays and into sinks, shouts of line cooks coordinating the timing of dishes, and the low din of seated diners. Standing there, I feel the aches and pains of joints that continue to stand by me, despite the years of unmerciful wear and tear I've put them through. They tell the story of a life filled with twelve- to fifteen-hour days that bleed into nights and sometimes straight into mornings.

There's no doubt about it, life as a restaurant chef is an utter assault on the senses. But when there's a rare break in service—a stolen moment to wipe the sweat from my brow, check the time, and breathe—I always look to the diners for whom it's all for. I see a table of four eagerly await their meals while laughing over a shared bottle of wine. A seated guest looks up to his waiter in a moment of counsel. My eyes pass over the empty plates left behind by satisfied eaters. I see regulars telling neighborhood stories at the bar. And sometimes, just sometimes, I'm lucky enough to tune in at just the moment that a smile erupts in approval of a first bite. And in these moments the pandemonium fades to the background and I am at peace, completely in my element, blissfully in the zone as I pump out orders. Recharged with the reminder of why I cook. The freedom of creativity, the gratification of having produced something delicious, and the infectious joy that can spread.

Like so many of my fellow chefs, I thrive under the pressure of the kitchen. My affection for the unrelenting mayhem is how I know that I do what I love, and I feel grateful for that. And so it might follow that if I'm unfazed by a night of three hundred covers or a round in Kitchen Stadium on *Iron Chef,* then a small dinner party at home would be child's play. But once plucked out of my comfortable stainless-steel surroundings and landed on the other side, in the place of home cook, I become anxious, and my anxiety leads to dread. The all-consuming energy and excitement that are with me throughout service, cooking demos, and even on-air cooking competitions somehow escape me in my home kitchen.

The ability to put dinner on the table seven nights a week at home should not be underestimated—it's one of the hardest things to do, and it's why I have so much respect and admiration for all you home cooks out there! So, I'll just come right out and say it—my name is Amanda Freitag, executive chef, and I'm scared of cooking at home!

How can my passion at work be such a stumbling block at home? How can I easily knock out fabulous four-star meals in my restaurant kitchen, yet so often find myself staring blankly into my open home fridge or thumbing through a stack of take-out menus? I'll tell you how. It's because after years and years of restaurant cooking, I became so accustomed to the familiar rhythms of cooking as part of a team that I lost sight of what it meant to cook for myself and by myself in what suddenly seemed to be an extremely tiny and ill-equipped kitchen. At work I always have expansive work surfaces, never-ending shelves and racks of equipment, and a team of chefs who help make it all happen, and suddenly it was just me, myself, and I.

Since I started my cooking journey as part of a kitchen brigade, this was a first for me. I rarely cooked at home before culinary school. When I was a kid, I watched my parents cook—but it wasn't a romantic, gauze-filtered experience. They both worked and were often tight on time when it came to meals. Growing up in New Jersey, my brothers and I were latchkey kids who took care of our own snacks and, sometimes, dinners. Weeknight meals were whatever was quickest and easiest. Sunday dinners and holidays were more elaborate; my parents had a bit more time to cook, so we'd all sit down to eat a meal that felt more special.

The culinary world may have been foreign to my parents, but they were wonderfully supportive of my career choice, as was my high school home ec teacher, and so I had the great fortune of attending the Culinary Institute of America. After high school I headed straight into professional kitchens and training and never looked back. Like my peers, I climbed my way up the ladder working endless hours to hone my craft in the restaurant world and devoted my time to learning as much as I could about the industry. With all the hours spent learning and working to be a successful executive chef, I didn't really have the time for cooking at home. The ovens in the string of tiny New York City apartments I've lived in throughout my career were rarely, if ever, turned on.

This all changed a couple of years ago, when I found myself with time off between restaurants and realized that I could take a breath or two. With my newfound free time, I attempted to cook at home—but I felt like a stranger in a strange kitchen. Where were the pots and pans? Yikes! It dawned on me that I had kind of skipped the whole home-cooking thing. I had no clue about how to really cook for myself or a crowd at home—let alone how to enjoy myself while doing it!

In the quiet solitude of my small home kitchen, I lost my confidence and my motivation. I used my lack of space, equipment, and ingredients as an excuse. I felt overwhelmed. I never had friends over for dinner parties. I was always a happy volunteer in other people's kitchens but never the holiday host for family get-togethers. My take-out menus were worn thin. I had to snap myself out of it. I wanted to be able to put the same smiling faces I see on my restaurant diners on the faces of my friends and family and cook delicious food in the comfort of my home kitchen!

So I did what I've always done in the face of fear, ever since my first scary days of culinary school and restaurant work—I hit it face-on. I went back to the drawing board. I dug deep and reminded myself that I cook because I love to experiment and create delicious food, and I can do that anywhere. It's not the kitchen that makes the food—it's the cook. And now that I'm on the other side, I've realized that an array of hurdles can make home cooking seem like you're trying to get through an obstacle course—but it doesn't have to be that way. With a few professional, confidence-instilling tricks up your sleeve, what was once daunting can become easier. And maybe even fun!

In this book I've collected the most helpful and reliable tips and tricks I've learned throughout my many years of working in professional restaurant kitchens. I realized that if items like caramelized onions and shallot confit and creamy risotto can help get me out of a pinch or add a burst of flavor in a restaurant kitchen, then why not start relying on them at home, too? That's why I've included them, among others in the "Back to Basics" chapter, to arm you with the foundational building blocks that have helped me in my kitchen. In the chapter "What's for Dinner?," I've compiled my favorite meals for weeknights or time-crunched weekends—they're steadfast without being boring. My "Pork on Pork" Chops and "Lusty" Lemon Chicken are a couple of my proudest creations, so of course they show up here. Many of the recipes come from my fellow cooks and chefs—those I've worked for, been taught by, eaten with, judged on TV, and even competed against. The recipes, tips, and stories here make it a sort of scrapbook, each recipe triggering a memory of a friend, fellow chef, relative (my dad's beef stew), meal, ingredient (my obsession with quinoa), or moment that has made a lasting impact. They've helped me find the love for cooking in my home kitchen and my hope is that you'll be able to make them your own, so they'll do the same for you.

A PRO RECIPE FOR SUCCESS

A lot of cookbooks start out by giving a lengthy list of "must-have" ingredients and equipment. Not only am I not going to do that, but I want you to focus on the few tools that you really need—and you can't find them in a store, which is a bonus because they'll cost you nothing. And you already have access to them in your kitchen. They're the pro tips and tricks that will get you into the executive chef mind-set—because just thinking like a chef is more than half the battle. The real chef tools that will offer the courage you need to be fearless in your own kitchen are *flexibility, organization,* and *confidence.* These are the most vital tools you'll find in every pro chef's kitchen, not shiny, expensive, high-powered tools, an exotic spice cabinet, or an expensive olive oil collection. There's no doubt that these things are

As you can see, my kitchen is the opposite of large, with a junk drawer! And far from professionally equipped.

helpful to have around the kitchen, but the reality is that you most likely already have everything you need to find success and joy in your home kitchen. For example, your hands are often your best tools. You don't need ten different pots and pans. As basic as it gets, rubber spatulas and wooden spoons work wonders. I promise you—the size of your kitchen should not make or break you.

Flexibility, organization, and confidence—these are the ingredients you really need, and they're what I relied on to get me cooking at home.

FLEXIBILITY

I won't pretend that the tricks an executive chef learns in culinary school or coming up the ranks of restaurant kitchens are earth-shattering, but they do drive home some very important habits that change the way we approach cooking—including the ability to adapt under pressure or change course. Cracks in this basic foundation are enough to have a conceptually sound dish completely collapse. I see it happen all the time when I judge *Chopped* and have had to avoid the same pitfalls when competing on *The Next Iron Chef*. Being tethered to an initial concept or ingredient list will see you fail when you hit a snag, which is usually inevitable, and it will limit what you believe you can achieve in your kitchen. Flexibility keeps your options open, so that just when you think it's time to bail, you'll make a small adjustment and stay the course.

In a restaurant kitchen, never is this flexibility more key than when it comes to ingredient availability. In an ideal world, the fish guy would always show up with the haddock that I ordered, but sometimes the fishermen just didn't catch the haddock. Or the delivery doesn't arrive in time. Or someone forgot to place the order. Or it was delivered, but the fridge in which it was stored broke down overnight and we had to get rid of it. Or any one of countless mishaps that can come to pass in a restaurant kitchen has happened. I don't, and can't, panic and close the doors each time I encounter a setback. Well, sometimes I might panic just a little.

But after the initial freak-out is over, I reassess, adjust, and move on, working with what I have or changing the menu item completely—whatever needs to be done to get back on course. This flexibility is ultimately what prevents complete kitchen meltdowns, and the more adaptable you can be, the more confident a cook you will become.

Knowledge is power in the kitchen—especially when you want to have more flexibility. So when you hit an ingredient snag, stop to think a little bit about what that ingredient is contributing to the dish. Is it texture? Is it flavor? Is it both? In some cases you can hack an ingredient. For example, if you're without Worcestershire sauce, maybe you have the components to create something very similar: soy sauce, molasses, anchovy paste, sugar, salt, garlic, and vinegar. Or, if you're all out of brown sugar, don't cancel your baking plans—just combine molasses with white sugar and you're back on track. Same with buttermilk—combine milk with a bit of lemon juice when you're pressed. For the many cases where you can't create something similar, try replacing it completely. If you can't find shallots in the grocery store, maybe use a small red onion instead. Greek yogurt, sour cream, and crème fraîche are basically interchangeable. This is just the beginning of all the substitutions that are possible in any given recipe. I could write an entire book on just substitutions and replacements. If you find yourself in this situation, and you really can't think of a way around it, do a quick Internet search and chances are you'll find something! Seriously, unless it's the absolute focal point of a dish—for example, the chicken in the "Lusty" Lemon Chicken recipe—there is rarely a reason for you to get discouraged when you find yourself without a particular ingredient. Just adapt and move on.

Beyond ingredients, one of the things that had me so scared about cooking at home after years of professional cooking was how tiny and ill-equipped my kitchen felt. No sous vide machine? No high-powered range? No convection oven? In my restaurant kitchens, pots and pans and spoons and ladles and spacious, glistening stainless-steel worktops are everywhere you look. Space and tools have never been a problem. At home, I felt that what I had was insufficient. But I soon realized that I had become too comfortable with the stockpile of tools and equipment that make it easy for me to cook in pro kitchens. So I got back to basics. I worked with what I had, and while it was a tight squeeze for sure, I was still able to cook challenging and restaurant-quality dishes at home.

Some things you can't get around, so, yes, you pretty much always need a knife. An oven is helpful, too. But you'd be surprised how much of what we have (or think we need) in our kitchens is either superfluous or unnecessary. Yes, it's nice to have a very heavy-bottomed Dutch oven for searing and braising. But is it necessary to spend $400 on a particular porcelain-enameled Dutch oven to create amazing braised short ribs? No. Chances are that whatever big ol' pot you've been using will do the job just fine. I have one 12-inch skillet that I use for pretty much everything that I make at home. It's my go-to pan. I own a heavy, expensive stand mixer—and it lives on the floor, collecting dust in my tiny New York City kitchen. It's so awkward and heavy that I rarely put it in action—because pretty much anything I would use it for is possible to do by hand or another way. I even fashioned a slotted spoon out of tin foil while cooking on a beach in an episode of *The Next Iron Chef*, which basically proves that a little ingenuity goes quite a long way in cooking.

Don't get me wrong—if given the choice between a tin foil slotted spoon and an actual slotted spoon, I would have chosen the real deal. But, while momentarily stressful for sure, it's often in these moments that I find you can put your own stamp on what you cook, allowing your creativity to really shine through. Take the classic tarte tatin. Legend has it that the now quintessentially French dessert was created by accident after a cook in France, attempting to make a traditional apple tart, overcooked the apples to the point of no return. In an effort to rescue the failing tart, she slapped the pastry crust on top of the pan and finished baking it upside-down. The result was delicious and creative and the diners ate it, none the wiser—probably assuming it was the full intent of the chef to create this wonderful new spin on a classic dessert. And the now-classic tarte tatin was born—out of a mistake! Food history is full of dishes created out of necessity when the original plan or recipe went awry or wasn't possible. After all, necessity is the mother of invention, it's not the mother of throwing in the towel to walk away and order a pizza.

Thinking on your feet means removing any reason that you "can't" or "won't" get in that kitchen and cook, so get in there and take some risks, because with a little flexibility and ingenuity, there's almost always a way around it!

ORGANIZATION

Now that you're hopefully feeling flexible enough to adapt rather than flee under pressure, let's talk about organization.

When it comes to recipes, take a professional approach. This means using them as a guide rather than a firm set of instructions, and prepping your ingredients before any of them come close to the heat. I often say that I don't use recipes, which is true to the extent that I don't read every word of a recipe and I never ever execute one without freestyling and putting my own stamp on it. Here's what I do when I open up a cookbook: Look at the cover, open it up, look at some pictures, speed-read the index, find a dish that piques my interest. Flip to the page and look at the picture, if there is one. Skim, skim, skim the recipe, studying the ingredient list, perusing the procedure, taking mental inventory of what I have on hand and what I need to do and what kind of time it requires, and then I prep. And while I cannot speak for every chef in the world, I can speak for many, many chefs I know when I say that most chefs do not use recipes as a step-by-step guide. We use them for inspiration and suggestions.

While I may not read every word of a recipe's procedure, by the time I begin to peel and dice I've definitely looked over the entire recipe so that I have some idea of what needs to be done before I fire up the burners. As an experienced chef, I already know about the timing and the prep. I can understand by looking at the bones of a recipe what's going to take four minutes versus an hour. And this is another big difference between your average home cook and a professional chef—if you can understand the hidden cues about timing and prep that are between the lines in the ingredient list and the procedure, then you can be even better prepared to know what you're in for and how to navigate the recipe to suit your timing. You can control the recipe rather than the recipe controlling you.

I feel so strongly about this shift in mind-set—getting away from viewing recipes as hard-and-fast rules for a dish—that I racked my brain for this book to try to come up with another word for them. My gut was to just totally throw away the word *recipe* altogether and replace it with *guideline* or *inspiration*. If I could, I'd never use the word *recipe* again, because in my experience at cooking demos and teaching classes all over the country, it seems only to inhibit the home cook, instilling immediate anxiety that you won't have the skill, or the ingredients, or the tools needed to complete a particular dish. But if you can liberate yourself from the idea of a recipe as a rigid assignment, you might unlock more space for creativity and fun in your cooking—and even invent the next tarte tatin.

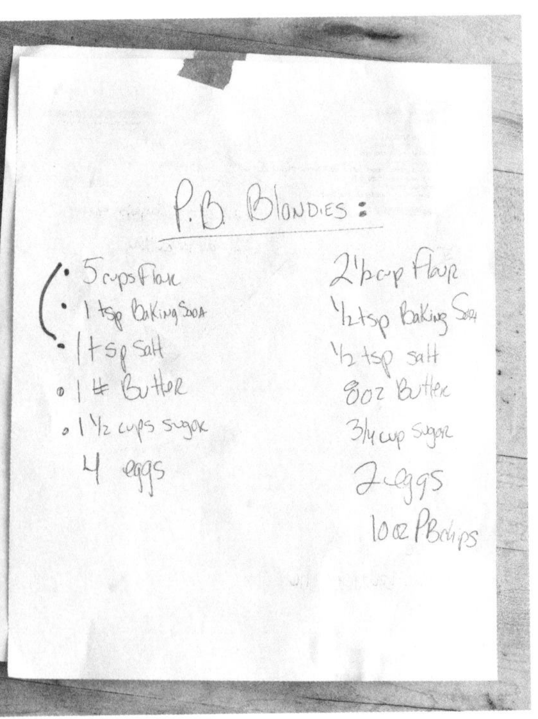

But while it's true that I don't use recipes in the traditional sense, like many of my friends in the industry I still own a slew of cookbooks, and I refer to them often. When I'm looking for inspiration, either at home or at the restaurant, I look to this cookbook collection, filled with pictures, words, and flavor combinations that get my creative juices flowing. My favorites rotate with time and trends and moods, but *Whole Larder Love* by Rohan Anderson and Yotam Ottolenghi's *Jerusalem* are leading the pack of my current favorites. Then there are the classics, the oldies but goodies, like *Joy of Cooking*—growing up, it was my go-to book, and it still sometimes is! Cookbook recipes, restaurant meals, and culinary travel help chefs brush the cobwebs off stale dishes and breathe new life into their cuisine. There's nothing like another cook's perspective to alter your own. And since the world of food is ever evolving, it is a great way to stay on top of trends in techniques and ingredients. I'm no different.

They say that in literature there are no new stories, only fresh twists, and food is similar. So, don't get me wrong, recipes are important. They teach technique and infuse new ideas that keep the food world fresh and constantly developing. I just want to inspire home cooks to start using recipes the way chefs do, as inspiration and motivation to get into the kitchen and cook.

Part of understanding the big picture at the beginning means breaking down the recipe until you can see the components that need to come together in order to end up with that delicious end result, kind of like you would a jigsaw puzzle. When I was a kid I would stare at the picture printed on the box in order to understand where the pieces needed to fit together. It's the same in cooking. Try to consider what parts of the puzzle need to be prepped and grouped together in order to put the final dish together. Do the onions and garlic need to be chopped? Does the dough need to be rested? Does anything need to be blanched or parboiled? If both your main course and the side dish require thyme leaves, why not pick them all at once? Considering the individual components of the recipe and prepping them will save time and energy and stress and change your cooking process for the better. I cannot emphasize enough the importance of organization and prep in the kitchen, no matter how easy or difficult the recipe. I don't begin to make even something as simple as pancake batter at home before setting myself up for it.

This is the seriously *big* chef tip that is often mentioned, and it's the reason professional chefs can cook at the level they do. Prepping ingredients before you begin cooking is not just a little tip that you can take or leave—it's the one technique that will change everything about the way you cook. In restaurant kitchens we make prep lists—and I do this religiously at home now, too. I break down a recipe, understand how the components need to be prepped, make a list, and work my way through it.

To try to help you get into that same executive chef mind-set, I've made prep lists for the recipes in this book, too. Prep lists and organization are so important to professional cooking that of course there's a French term for it—*mise en place,* which means "put in place." Before you begin cooking, you have your *mise en place* ready to go—individual ingredients are prepped, blanched, cut, peeled, diced, sautéed. The necessary components for the final product are all there, neat and organized in front of you, ready to be put into action. The extra time spent on *mise en place* will save time in the end.

In the restaurant, once the "*mise*" is prepped, we put it all into individual "six" pans—square metal containers of various depths that are perfectly sized to be held in the refrigerated prep table, or heated line, or underneath the prep table in the "low boy" fridge—so that everything's on hand when it's needed. Larger items go into bigger hotel pans and liquids like stocks and soups go into large plastic containers, which go into walk-in fridges. No matter in what container food is stored, it gets slapped with a piece of masking tape on the side and labeled so it's visible immediately. That label always includes what it is and the date it was prepped or made.

I can only dream about this setup at home! But I still apply a lot of what we do in the restaurant at home—just scaled down. In my tiny home kitchen, I place all my advance prep, well labeled, in small pint or Tupperware containers or jars with lids and stack them neatly in my fridge and freezer. In the restaurant everything needs to be labeled all the time, but at home I don't bother labeling things I'm going to use right away—just the sauces and vinaigrettes and stocks that I make in large quantities, or elements of dishes that I make ahead of time. It's worth it to collect various size jars and plastic containers with lids, so that you can use the smallest practical container. You don't need to make a large investment in the containers—just take the labels off jam jars or mason jars, for example. If you label the side, rather than the top, you won't need to rummage through each stack you've neatly created in search of the ingredient you need—you'll see it right away. The tighter the space you have to work with, the more important it is to be prepped and organized ahead of time. I realized this once I got serious about cooking at home.

Once the prep is done, then the cooking can begin—but not before.

CONFIDENCE

I definitely lost my mojo when I was transplanted to my home kitchen. Kitchen Stadium? No problem. A restaurant packed to the gills with hungry diners and maybe even a restaurant critic or two? Bring it on. One hundred square feet of tiny home kitchen? Now *that* made me nervous. Suddenly I felt out of my element, and when your confidence is out of whack, that's the beginning of the end in the kitchen.

In my home kitchen, underconfidence was one of my issues. But overconfidence in the kitchen can be just as detrimental. Maybe you had a particular time frame in which to get your cooking done and you didn't plan accordingly—and timing is everything. Or perhaps you were feeling feisty and inspired to attempt a new dish for company, but got ahead of yourself and attempted a whole new menu, with every course or dish involving a new technique or ingredient. If your meal isn't a success, that kind of ambition can make you want to abandon your kitchen altogether. Rest assured that the most celebrated chef can still make these mistakes, and as I see on *Chopped* all of the time, overconfidence can lead to your demise.

On the other hand, underconfidence might keep you from trying a new technique or working with a seemingly scary ingredient, such as artichokes. Or if you feel you don't have the right tools, or space, or time, or energy, or ingredients to produce a fabulous meal, you might become just as paralyzed as I did.

But if you have a plan, remain flexible and realistic about time, and create a well-organized prep list, the confidence will come naturally because you'll be prepared for the best and the worst and everything in between. And that's really the name of the game when it comes to cooking. Whether it's in a restaurant, a TV cooking competition, or your own home kitchen, the rules and foundations are the same. Sticking with them will enable you to break free from recipes, eventually becoming confident enough to make substitutions and create your own dishes. You'll be able to replicate and reinvent dishes and flavors you experience out at your favorite restaurants, or on your next travel adventure, just like the pros. My hope is that, like me, stepping into your kitchen to make a meal for one or two or four or ten will bring pleasure and joy rather than anxiety, because you'll know and remember the tricks of the trade.

I intentionally set up this book so that many of the less intimidating recipes are toward the front of the book. "The Scary Stuff" is exactly what it sounds like—recipes that involve techniques or ingredients that I think can sometimes seem too hard or scary for a home cook to attempt at home. That's not the case! I can understand the need to build your confidence, though—so while I encourage you to try every recipe in the "Scary Stuff"chapter (I think you'll surprise yourself), if you're feeling a little daunted, start out with some of the recipes in the "Low and Slow" or "What's for Dinner?" chapters. The "Sauces, Marinades, and Other Flavor Secrets" chapter is filled with recipes that will add lots of flavor to dishes that you might otherwise already feel comfortable with and have in your repertoire—try the Curry Golden Raisin Sauce on a simple piece of poached fish or grilled chicken, or the Rosemary-Anchovy Rub on a leg of lamb or roast beef.

No matter where you begin or what cooking ups and downs you might encounter, just remember that I struggled at home, too. I'll be there to help you along the way!

BACK TO BASICS

Just as I had to do when I started cooking at home, we're going to start at the beginning. No matter how fancy and progressive the restaurant or cuisine, certain building blocks and foundational skills and recipes come forward time and time again. They are the multitasking recipes that we chefs commit to memory from the outset of our careers. In fact, they're not really "recipes" as much as cooking habits, just as brushing your teeth is a ritual, an essential task that you complete mindlessly every day. Brushing your teeth is a necessary part of your routine, and for a chef, these basics are just as second nature.

They might not be the most exciting recipes, but these important staples are the workhorses that will get you out of a pinch every time. Add roasted garlic to make mashed potatoes pop with a little more depth of flavor. A simple equation of caramelized onions plus sherry plus stock equals the basis for a very unfussy French onion soup. If you had nothing but Arborio rice, a box of stock, an onion, and some butter, you could proudly host an impromptu dinner party. Throw in some reconstituted porcinis and their liquid and you become a star chef. If I were stuck on a desert island and could only bring my trusty sauté pan and one ingredient, I would choose eggs. Well, eggs, and also chocolate. In fact, I am *not* regularly stuck on a desert island, only in my teeny-tiny New York City apartment, and I still choose eggs! Almost every night for dinner, actually. I often put a simple fried egg on top of whatever leftover veggie side dish happens to be taking up real estate in my fridge. Paired with crusty bread or a simple side salad, it becomes a revived and balanced meal.

When armed with the clear knowledge and know-how of the basics, any cook or chef can venture into the kitchen with confidence, which is half the battle both at home and in the restaurant kitchen. Lesson number one in how to build confidence in the kitchen—get to know the basics. Because no matter what, there are always eggs!

Back to Basics

BASIC RISOTTO

MAKES 4 SERVINGS

When made correctly, risotto is really a perfect comfort food. Warm, creamy, and indulgent, it suits almost any occasion. Gussied up with porcinis or lobster, it makes an intimate dinner for two. When it's made in the classic and unfussy style, you have a cheap but impressive way to feed a family or guests. It isn't an amazing amount of skill or training that gives you great risotto. The big "secret" to risotto is using hot stock. Well, that and a little TLC. Have you been looking for an opportunity to get lost in your thoughts? Make risotto. Add stock. Stir. Daydream. Repeat.

- 4 cups Chicken Stock (page 27) or vegetable stock, plus more as needed
- 1 tablespoon unsalted butter
- 1 Spanish onion, diced
- 1 cup Arborio rice
- Kosher salt and freshly cracked black pepper
- Grated Parmesan cheese

PREP: PEEL AND DICE THE ONION

1. Pour the stock into a small saucepan and set it over low heat.
2. Melt the butter in a medium saucepan over low heat. Add the onion and season with a pinch of salt. Sauté the onion until it's translucent, 6 to 8 minutes, making sure it doesn't brown.
3. Add the rice and stir, coating the rice completely with the butter.
4. Add 1 cup of the hot stock to the rice. Stir and simmer the rice over medium-low heat until all the stock has been absorbed.
5. Add another cup of hot stock to the rice, repeating the process until the stock is gone and the rice is cooked. The only way to know if risotto is correctly done is to taste it! When you bite into a spoonful, each grain of

{ CONTINUED }

rice should be texturally well defined and al dente in the same manner as perfectly cooked pasta.

6. Season with salt and pepper to taste. Finish with grated Parmesan and serve.

---

* **Finished risotto should be neither soupy nor dry. You're looking for a middle consistency that celebrates the starchiness of the rice and is naturally creamy but not heavy or gloppy.**

* **If using store-bought stock, be sure to purchase a quality, low-sodium brand. Be extra careful with your seasoning in this case, tasting as you go, because a low-sodium stock isn't salt-free.**

* **My favorite risotto variations: saffron for a classic Milanese style, shrimp and peas, blanched asparagus for a celebration of spring, butternut squash and sage for a warming winter meal, or mixed mushroom and leek for an earthy foray into autumn.**

CARAMELIZED ONIONS

MAKES 2½ CUPS

This is kind of similar to the roasted garlic miracle on page 15. Slowly caramelizing onions removes their abrupt flavor and draws out the inherent sweetness that lies beneath this most basic and affordable of ingredients. As a pro chef, I'm also subject to kitchen budgets; we chefs are trained to work with the most humble ingredients and transform them into elegant and complex food that diners want to eat. We can't always look to the most expensive and exotic ingredients. Anyone can make filet mignon taste great, but the challenge lies in trying to create something exciting and delicious from what the budget allows, and sometimes that's onions.

¼ cup extra-virgin olive oil

3 large Spanish onions, peeled and sliced

½ teaspoon kosher salt

PREP: PEEL, CORE, AND SLICE THE ONIONS

1. In a 14-inch skillet, heat the olive oil over high heat. Add the sliced onions. Do *not* stir or shake the pan after the onions are added; just let the heat of the pan recover from adding the onions. Listen for a sizzling noise to return.
2. Season the onions with salt and begin to stir. You should see that the onions on the bottom, which hit the pan first, will have already started to brown.
3. Turn the heat down to medium and keep cooking, stirring occasionally, for 15 minutes. The onions will begin to soften and release their juices. This is exactly what you want to happen, so that you can caramelize the onions' natural sugars.
4. Turn the heat down to low and cook, periodically stirring to make sure the onions don't burn on the bottom, for another 30 minutes, or until they are completely soft and a rich dark brown color.

{ CONTINUED }

5. Transfer the onions to a separate bowl to cool. After they have completely cooled, store them in an airtight container in the refrigerator.

* **These basic caramelized onions can have so many uses. They make a great burger or sandwich topping, and with the addition of wine or sherry can quickly turn into a sauce for beef, or a French onion soup on a cold night. Or even throw them into a Saturday-morning frittata or scrambled eggs for added flavor.**

* **I prefer Spanish onions as my go-to, universal onion because white onions are often far too astringent and can easily overpower a dish.**

–French Onion Soup

Combine 1 recipe caramelized onions, 1 teaspoon fresh thyme leaves, 2 cups beef stock, and 1/4 cup sherry in a medium saucepan. Stir and season with salt and pepper. Cook for 1 hour, uncovered, over medium-low heat. Taste and season. Divide among two or three soup crocks and top with croutons (Caesar Salad, page 89) and shredded Gruyère. Broil until bubbling and golden brown.

BASIC BLANCHED VEGETABLES

I'm sure if you've ever watched *Chopped* or almost any other food TV show, you've seen chefs blanch and then "shock" their cooked vegetables before using them in a dish. Blanching (cooking quickly in boiling water) gives vegetables a head start on cooking, while shocking them in ice water instantly stops the cooking and allows the vegetable to retain its vibrant color and perfectly cooked texture. The importance of blanching your vegetables should not be underestimated; what seems like an extraneous step actually ends up saving you time and chaos when you're putting together your final dish or meal. Think of it as heavy-duty *mise en place* (see page xvii). The heavy pot of boiling water will be off the stovetop and the veggies will be sitting nicely cooked and colorful ready to be sautéed, dressed, grilled, or whatever their final cooking destiny may be.

1. Bring 1 gallon salted water to a boil in a large pot.

2. Prepare a large bowl with equal parts ice and water for "shocking" the vegetables.

3. Trim the fibrous or woody ends from vegetables like broccolini, broccoli rabe, and asparagus. For asparagus, if you're not sure how far up on the stalk to trim, test one by bending back the end piece. Where it snaps off naturally is where you should cut. Peel or trim as needed for other vegetables like broccoli, cauliflower, green beans, and carrots. Loose peas can just be tossed in!

4. Place the vegetables in the boiling water. After 45 seconds (exactly), remove them with a slotted spoon, spider, or tongs and plunge them straight into the prepared ice bath. Green vegetables should have a brilliant green color. Once they're cooled, remove them from the ice water and lay them on paper towels to drain thoroughly.

   Note: *Blanching and shocking start and stop the cooking process and lock in your desired texture while also helping presentation by*

{ CONTINUED }

encouraging green vegetables to retain their vibrant hue. The same process is applicable to any vegetable that needs a head start before being used in the final recipe. Cauliflower, carrots, and turnips are good examples. Keep in mind that sturdier vegetables like cauliflower and carrots will need a bit longer in order to really precook. If you want crunchy, toothsome vegetables, then the 45- to 60-second guideline is a good rule of thumb. The goal of blanching is never to fully cook, but to partially cook as part of your prep list in the beginning of a lot of recipes.

* **Use this technique for Asparagus Salad with Parmesan (page 98), Broccolini with Lemon and Rosemary (page 194), or Green Beans with Toasted Almonds (page 185).**

OVEN-ROASTED TOMATOES

MAKES 8 TOMATO HALVES

I want tomatoes on my burgers and salads all year round. But alas, here in New York City I'm tied to the tomato season, which dictates that I can only eat and serve fresh tomatoes between July and September. In order to satisfy my cravings and free myself from seasonal constraints, I oven-roast tomatoes and keep them on hand at all times. So many chefs for whom I've worked have used this technique; the seasonings may vary but it's all the same idea: to intensify flavor by roasting. Removing the moisture leads to a stronger, more concentrated flavor that renders otherwise watery, flavorless, out-of-season tomatoes edible and delicious.

4 beefsteak tomatoes, halved horizontally

1 tablespoon extra-virgin olive oil

⅛ teaspoon kosher salt

⅛ teaspoon freshly cracked black pepper

1 teaspoon fresh thyme leaves, chopped

PREP: HALVE THE TOMATOES • CHOP THE THYME LEAVES

1. Preheat the oven to 300°F and make sure the oven rack is in the center position. Line a baking sheet with aluminum foil.
2. Place the tomatoes cut side up on the prepared baking sheet. Drizzle the olive oil over the tomatoes. Season the tomatoes with the salt, pepper, and thyme.
3. Roast the tomatoes for 1½ to 2 hours, or until they have shrunk by 50 percent and are starting to wrinkle and intensify in color.
4. Let the tomatoes cool completely, then place them in an airtight container and refrigerate.

* These tomatoes will keep for up to one week and can be added to practically any dish you can think of! They're great in egg scrambles, in vinaigrettes, in sauces, in pastas, as a vegetable garnish, on a sandwich ... the possibilities are endless.

with
Shallot Confit
(page 16)

ROASTED GARLIC

MAKES 4 HEADS

Roasted garlic is the best! It's a miraculous transformation of an ingredient that when raw can be harsh and spicy, but once roasted becomes a sweet, spreadable version of itself—offering a completely different flavor and texture. Roasting garlic is an illustration of how the simplest techniques and ingredients can still be versatile and complex. So many cultures around the world routinely employ garlic in their cuisine, so knowing how to make and use roasted garlic can offer infinite opportunities for playing with your favorite recipes. Roasting garlic takes a completely ordinary, everyday, universal ingredient and throws it on its head—in such a simple and straightforward way. Just when you thought you knew garlic, meet its roasted relative.

4 whole garlic heads

2 tablespoons olive oil

⅛ teaspoon kosher salt

Salt draws the natural juices from aromatics and vegetables, intensifying the flavor.

1. Preheat the oven to 375°F.
2. Place the garlic heads on their side, so that the root and tip are horizontal to your cutting board. Using a serrated knife, carefully cut off the tops of the garlic heads, about ¼ inch from the tip, exposing the cloves but not so far down that they fall apart.
3. Place all the garlic heads cut side up in the center of a piece of aluminum foil large enough to contain them all. Drizzle the garlic heads with the olive oil and season them with the salt.
4. Bring the edges of the foil over the garlic heads to make a sealed pouch. You can place this in a small baking dish or directly on the oven rack.
5. Bake for 45 to 50 minutes, then check to see if the garlic is tender and roasted by opening the foil and inserting a toothpick or skewer into the cloves. If the toothpick easily slides in and out, the garlic is ready. If needed, roast the garlic for another 5 minutes or so.

{ CONTINUED }

6. Let the package cool for a few minutes before opening the foil, as very hot steam will emerge. When the garlic is cool enough to handle safely, you can either squeeze the cloves into an airtight container or store them whole. To puree, squeeze the cloves directly onto your cutting board, discarding the papery skins. Smash the cloves with the back of a large spoon, a rubber spatula, or the flat of your knife, and voilà—roasted garlic puree!

* **My favorite uses for roasted garlic puree: mashed potatoes, crostini, pesto, pasta sauces, pizza, eggs, burger patties, chicken breasts, vinaigrettes, cream sauces, stir-fries, dips, and stews.**

SHALLOT CONFIT

MAKES 4 CUPS, WITH COOKING LIQUID

Confit is definitely a "cheffy" technique, and its French name makes it seem much more involved than it is. Its simplicity only adds to the elegance of the final product. Traditionally, *confit* means "cooked in its own fat"—as in duck or pork confit—but it can also mean cooking food, submerged in oil, slowly over low heat. You can pair shallot confit with fish or meat and add it to salads, using the oil it is cooked in for the vinaigrette.

7 or 8 whole shallots, peeled and trimmed

1 cup extra-virgin olive oil

¾ cup canola oil

2 fresh thyme sprigs

⅛ teaspoon kosher salt

1 teaspoon whole black peppercorns

PREP: PEEL AND TRIM THE SHALLOTS, BUT LEAVE THEM WHOLE

1. Place all the ingredients in a small saucepan (choose one that allows the shallots to be covered in oil while not allowing it to bubble over; add a bit more oil if necessary). Bring to a simmer over medium heat. Turn the heat down to very low and cook for 25 to 30 minutes, or until the shallots are completely tender and easily pierced with the tip of a paring knife.

* **The shallots will last for up to two weeks if they're submerged in the oil and refrigerated.**

* **When you're looking for a subtle onion flavor with a little sweetness, shallots are the onion for you! They're widely available—not always in the bulk onion and garlic section, but sometimes sneakily hidden near the refrigerated herbs. When choosing shallots, look for a firm, intact skin free of visible bruises.**

* **Try this with whole peeled garlic cloves!**

FRESH PASTA DOUGH

MAKES 1 POUND

Every chef has a different pasta dough recipe—and I use the word *recipe* very loosely here; it's more of a ratio. They're all variations on a very similar theme, but you'll find that even subtle differences can make a big impact on texture and flavor. Some recipes call for eggs, others do not. While some chefs work only with the very highly refined "00" flour, others find all-purpose flour just fine. I prefer a combination of all-purpose and durum, which is a harder wheat, for the texture it gives to the finished product. The addition of either or both water and olive oil is also a personal choice. Although I have a few variations in my pocket, this is my go-to, all-around pasta dough. This recipe is kind of like a choose-your-own-adventure book, because you can make it by hand or in a food processor. The only difference will be how many calories you burn!

2½ cups all-purpose flour, plus more as needed

1 cup durum flour

1 teaspoon kosher salt

5 large eggs

2 teaspoons extra-virgin olive oil

HAND METHOD

1. In a large bowl or on a clean surface, use a fork to blend the flours and salt. Use your fist to make a well in the middle of the seasoned flour, ensuring that the flour is high enough on all sides that it will form a wall that prevents the eggs from running all over the place. Add the eggs and olive oil to the well. Use a fork to begin incorporating the flour into the eggs. Continue to bring flour into the eggs with the fork until the fork becomes difficult to maneuver.

2. Get in there with your clean hands and knead the dough, adding small amounts of water or flour until the ball of dough just comes together—it doesn't have to be silky smooth.

{ CONTINUED }

FOOD PROCESSOR METHOD

1. Combine all the ingredients in the bowl of a food processor and pulse until the dough comes together and pulls cleanly away from the sides of the food processor. If it looks like the dough is still sticking to the sides and is a little too dry to come together, add 1 tablespoon water and pulse.

2. Transfer the dough to a lightly floured surface and work the dough into a ball. It doesn't have to be silky smooth.

TO MAKE THE PASTA

1. You now have a unified ball of dough that might still have some cracks and divots throughout. Wrap the dough in plastic and let it rest in the fridge for at least 1 hour.

2. Set up a pasta sheeter—either a manual roller or a stand mixer attachment.

3. Remove the dough from the fridge, unwrap it, and cut it into four or five small sections. Use a rolling pin or the palm of your hand to flatten the sections so that they will fit easily into the pasta sheeter.

4. Beginning on the widest setting, roll the dough through the machine twice, folding it in half or thirds before you put it through the second time. Continue to move down the increments of the roller, folding it into a more manageable rectangle each time, decreasing in thickness, rolling only once at each stage. Stop at your desired thickness.

   Note: *If you're making stuffed pasta, such as ravioli or tortellini, continue to roll the pasta through to the last, thinnest setting. If you're making traditional cut pasta, such as fettuccine or spaghetti, stop rolling at your desired thickness.*

* A good visual cue for knowing you've achieved the pasta dough of your dreams is that when you cut into the raw ball of dough you should see tiny air bubbles and, if you look closely, ribbons of gluten that swirl through it.

* Many factors can influence handmade pasta on any given day, especially the humidity levels of the kitchen. The drier the air, the more egg and/or oil you might have to add. The more moisture in the air, the less moisture you'll need for the dough. So the best way to learn to make pasta dough is to know how it should look and feel—it will help you feel comfortable making adjustments to your ratios.

* While it's entirely possible to hand-roll your pasta sheets, it will take some time and some serious muscle! I do not recommend it, but if you're without either an electric sheeter or a manual roller and just can't live without homemade pasta, whip out your trusty rolling pin and get rolling! A handy tip is to rotate the dough after every roll; this will prevent it from sticking to your work surface. If you want to see how it's done, the web abounds with videos of very strong Italian mammas and grandmothers who put me to shame when it comes to hand-rolling!

VINAIGRETTES

There's a dizzying number of fancy (and not-so-fancy) vinaigrettes lining supermarket shelves these days. But once you finally select one from the shelf, you find that sugar is second on the ingredient list, or that half the list is additives and preservatives you can't pronounce. Making your own vinaigrettes is not only easy but saves money and gives you full control over the ingredients. All you need are five minutes and a mason jar. You can shake up a jar on Sunday and have it on hand for salads all week long. And, oh, the variety! Once you understand the standard ratio, which is usually one part acid to three parts oil, you can get as creative as you like with flavors and combinations, including everything from citrus juice, zest, herbs, spices, and cheeses, to name a few. I tend to enjoy more acidic vinaigrettes, so I stick to more of a one-to-two ratio, but that's just me! These are some of my go-to vinaigrettes—I think they represent a good cross section and are only the tip of the iceberg. Wink wink.

SHERRY TAPENADE VINAIGRETTE

MAKES 2 CUPS

I love olives! Here's the perfect excuse to consume them. Making tapenade is a cinch—but feel free to use a quality store-bought tapenade for this recipe. This recipe is meant to be thicker than your average vinaigrette and is perfect on a summertime tomato and arugula salad.

½ cup sherry vinegar

1¼ cups olive oil

⅛ teaspoon kosher salt

⅛ teaspoon freshly cracked black pepper

½ cup prepared black olive tapenade (or try making it—see below)

1. Whisk all the ingredients together in a bowl and store in a tightly sealed jar. Shake the jar to reemulsify before using.

Quick tapenade: 1 cup pitted black olives, 2 tablespoons capers, 1 large garlic clove, all finely minced or pulsed in a food processor. Add olive oil to cover.

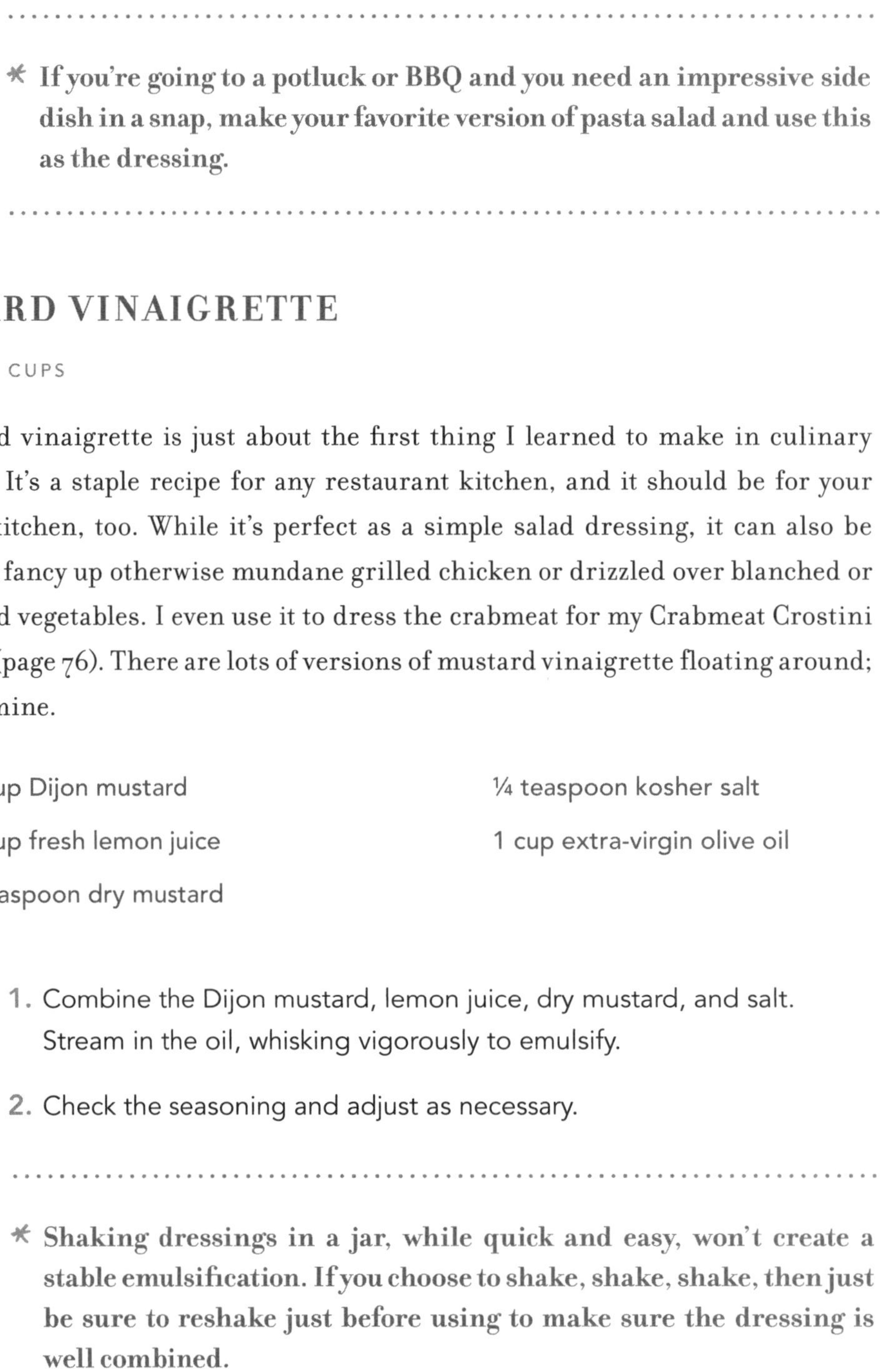

* **If you're going to a potluck or BBQ and you need an impressive side dish in a snap, make your favorite version of pasta salad and use this as the dressing.**

MUSTARD VINAIGRETTE

MAKES 1½ CUPS

Mustard vinaigrette is just about the first thing I learned to make in culinary school. It's a staple recipe for any restaurant kitchen, and it should be for your home kitchen, too. While it's perfect as a simple salad dressing, it can also be used to fancy up otherwise mundane grilled chicken or drizzled over blanched or steamed vegetables. I even use it to dress the crabmeat for my Crabmeat Crostini recipe (page 76). There are lots of versions of mustard vinaigrette floating around; here's mine.

¼ cup Dijon mustard
½ cup fresh lemon juice
1 teaspoon dry mustard
¼ teaspoon kosher salt
1 cup extra-virgin olive oil

1. Combine the Dijon mustard, lemon juice, dry mustard, and salt. Stream in the oil, whisking vigorously to emulsify.
2. Check the seasoning and adjust as necessary.

* **Shaking dressings in a jar, while quick and easy, won't create a stable emulsification. If you choose to shake, shake, shake, then just be sure to reshake just before using to make sure the dressing is well combined.**

Mustard is magical because it almost never fails to emulsify whatever vinaigrette or sauce you add it to.

WHITE BALSAMIC VINAIGRETTE

MAKES 2 CUPS

- 2 small garlic cloves, minced
- 2 teaspoons Dijon mustard
- ½ cup white balsamic vinegar
- 1½ cups extra-virgin olive oil
- ¼ teaspoon kosher salt
- ⅛ teaspoon freshly cracked black pepper

1. In a medium bowl, whisk together the garlic, mustard, and white balsamic vinegar.
2. Slowly stream in the olive oil while vigorously whisking to emulsify. Season with the salt and pepper.

TOMATO VINAIGRETTE

MAKES 2 CUPS

Here's a great dressing that uses the oven-roasted tomatoes and roasted garlic you may already have on hand from this chapter.

- ¼ cup balsamic vinegar
- ¼ cup red wine vinegar
- 1 shallot, thinly sliced
- 6 oven-roasted tomato halves, diced (see page 12)
- 1 teaspoon roasted garlic puree (see page 15)
- 1 teaspoon kosher salt
- ⅛ teaspoon freshly cracked black pepper
- ¾ cup extra-virgin olive oil

PREP: PEEL AND THINLY SLICE THE SHALLOT • CUT THE TOMATOES INTO SMALL DICE

1. Combine the vinegars in a small saucepan and bring to a boil over medium heat. Remove from the heat, add the shallot, and let steep for 15 minutes. Strain the mixture through a fine-mesh strainer into a medium bowl, discarding the shallot.
2. Add the tomatoes, garlic puree, salt, and pepper to the bowl and whisk to combine. Slowly stream in the oil while whisking to emulsify.

RED WINE VINAIGRETTE

MAKES 1 CUP

This is a classic vinaigrette that can be used on almost any salad. It's the perfect weekday vinaigrette—a go-to for when I'm throwing together a refrigerator-clearing salad for myself. The Italian herbs in this vinaigrette make it perfect for any salad that will be served with or before an Italian-inspired meal. Think Sunday Jersey meatballs and bitter tricolor salad!

- 1 garlic clove, minced
- ½ small shallot, minced
- 1 teaspoon dried thyme
- 1 teaspoon dried oregano
- ¼ cup red wine vinegar
- Kosher salt and freshly cracked black pepper, to taste
- ¾ cup extra-virgin olive oil

PREP: PEEL AND MINCE THE GARLIC AND SHALLOT

1. In a small bowl, whisk together all the ingredients, adding the olive oil last. You can also shake the dressing in a jar until it's emulsified.

*** A great addition to this vinaigrette is freshly grated Parmesan cheese, but adding the cheese will shorten the shelf life of the dressing, so add it as you need it unless you plan on using all the dressing at once.**

CHICKEN STOCK

MAKES 2½ QUARTS

Let's just get it out of the way first. Yes! I use store-bought stock, and I'm not ashamed to admit it! These days I feel appreciative if I can spare any kind of time at home to make my own chicken stock from scratch. However, this just very rarely seems to be the case. Our lives are busy, so let's embrace the help that premade stock offers the home cook in getting a wide array of tasty and healthy homemade dishes to the table. I'm sick and tired of reading about how store-bought stock is a second-rate shortcut when I think it has just become a modern-day reality for our harried lives and packed schedules. Homemade stock is a bonus.

So if you have time and freezer space, please give my basic chicken stock recipe a go. I love to brew up a big batch over the cold months to store in my fridge and freezer for warming soups, stocks, and risottos. Otherwise, if time is short, embrace the boxed stock—there are so many quality options out there (see page 28 for some things to look for). I will not be hiding my boxes of stock in the back of my teeny kitchen cabinets anymore. Front and center. Secret is out!

4 Spanish onions, halved

4 large carrots, peeled and coarsely chopped

2 celery stalks, cut into large dice

5 garlic cloves

5 pounds chicken bones

1 tablespoon whole black peppercorns

2 bay leaves

6 fresh thyme sprigs

15 fresh parsley stems

PREP: PEEL AND HALVE THE ONIONS • PEEL AND COARSELY CHOP THE CARROTS • DICE THE CELERY • PEEL THE GARLIC

1. Combine all the ingredients in a 5-gallon stockpot with 1½ gallons water. Make sure that the ingredients are covered with water.
2. Bring to a boil over high heat, uncovered, and use a ladle to skim off and discard any impurities that rise to the surface.

3. Turn the heat down so that the stock gently simmers and keep the stock at a simmer for 5 hours.

4. Strain the stock through a fine-mesh strainer, reserving the liquid and discarding the solids.

5. Portion the stock into workable units, as small or as large as you need for your cooking. For example, to add a flavor punch to simple rice or quinoa dishes, freeze individual portions in ice cube trays. Or for larger applications such as soup or risotto, store the stock in quart containers in the fridge or freezer, depending on when you will use it.

- **This is a very basic stock; feel free to add any spices or other aromatics as desired to build the flavor. For example, if you want to use your stock for a Vietnamese pho base, maybe add star anise and cinnamon. Or if you were thinking of making a Mexican tortilla soup, you could add fresh cilantro and ground cumin.**

- **When perusing the stock and broth section of your grocery store, make sure you keep an eye on the fine print on the boxes and cans. You should look for low-sodium options so you can have full control over the salt in your dishes. Also, check out the ingredient list and steer clear of stocks that contain sugar or MSG.**

SAUCES, MARINADES, AND OTHER FLAVOR SECRETS

Have you ever eaten in a restaurant and wondered, "How come my food never tastes like this? What's the chef's secret?" Ponder no more, because I'm about to let you in on it—the secret ingredients that allow restaurant food to taste as decadent and satisfying as it so often does are salt, fat, and time.

SALT

If you take away just one lesson from this book, let it be this: taste and season as you cook! Tasting along the way and adjusting your seasoning is an absolutely imperative step to finding the road to flavorful food. If you properly season as you go, the end result will taste neither salty nor bland—it will taste like the sum of its delicious parts. The carrots, onions, and celery you sauté to build a soup will impart their flavors and contribute to a much more complex finished product. Roasted chicken will deliver the crispy, golden skin of your dreams, while remaining moist and tasting divine.

A great way to become a more seasoned seasoner is to grab your salt with your fingers, not just shake a few meager grains through the teeny-tiny holes at the top of your saltshaker. Saltshakers and salt grinders are for the table, but hands are your most reliable tools while cooking. If your salt lives in a salt cellar, salt pig, or other moisture-free container—even a small Tupperware container with a lid—you can really get in there with your hands and understand the amount of salt you're about to add. Once you get a sense of how much salt you use in your dishes, you won't have to overthink it so much in the future. This is how chefs season "to taste"—you can't be strapped to measuring spoons in a fast-paced, high-volume kitchen.

FAT

Traditionally in restaurant cooking, we embrace butter, cream, bacon fat, duck fat, and other fats to maximize flavors. Eating out is often a special occasion, and we tend to treat ourselves without worrying too much about whether to indulge in the eggs Benedict dripping with hollandaise sauce. But home cooks think more about the long term, balancing the desire to make flavorful food with the need to factor in dietary concerns. Luckily we have spices, herbs, and aromatics such as garlic, onions, ginger, and lemongrass to help us create great flavor with less fat. So whether you're looking to slim down your meals or just have fun with bold flavors, spice rubs, quick sauces, and marinades can get you closer to the restaurant quality you strive for.

TIME

In our daily lives, we always seem to run out of time. It can happen in restaurants as well, where an entire brigade, all completing their individual tasks and prep, needs to work in concert so that everything is ready by the time service comes along. Meanwhile, that same team of chefs and cooks is thinking about menus one or two weeks or even a month in advance. Meats are sometimes marinated overnight. Sauces can be built over hours, beginning with a veal stock that cooks overnight and reduces the next day. Food ordering is done in advance and food is delivered directly to a restaurant door—we chefs don't go shopping to get it. All of this saves us time in a restaurant kitchen.

But when I have to cook at home, it's just me—a solo act. I do the planning, the food shopping, the prep, and the cooking, then I transition to front of house and do the place setting and entertaining, and then I finish up by doing the cleaning. And I suspect you do the same! This makes cooking at home infinitely more difficult than cooking in the restaurant. Who has time to make an eight-hour veal stock or marinate tomorrow night's dinner today?

The recipes in this chapter will give your food the flavor and appeal that you find in restaurant meals, without the need for a kitchen brigade and a week's vacation.

Sauces, Marinades, and Other Flavor Secrets

MARINARA SAUCE

MAKES 4 TO 6 CUPS

When I was a kid, all I knew was marinara in a jar. Both of my parents worked, so they were superbusy and had to feed us kids in a hurry! But this sauce is just as easy to make as it is to buy. Yes, it takes close to an hour to cook, but you don't have to babysit it—throw the ingredients into a pot when you get home from work and by the time you set the table, throw in a load of laundry, put together a salad, and gather the family, it's time to cook and drain the pasta, and dinner is ready. And don't ever just make enough for one night! Make a double batch, throw it in the freezer, and use the leftovers later in the week or for weeks to come.

1 large onion, diced

3 garlic cloves, diced

¼ teaspoon chili flakes

2 tablespoons olive oil

¼ cup white wine

2 (28-ounce) cans whole plum tomatoes

1 tablespoon kosher salt

2 fresh basil leaves

½ tablespoon dried oregano

PREP: PEEL AND DICE THE ONION AND GARLIC • PICK THE BASIL LEAVES

1. In a large heavy-bottomed pot over medium heat, sauté the onion, garlic, and chili flakes in the olive oil until translucent and fragrant, 6 to 8 minutes.
2. Add the white wine and cook until the liquid has reduced by half.
3. Add the plum tomatoes and their juices, the salt, basil leaves, and oregano and stir well.
4. Use a potato masher, whisk, or hand blender to break down the tomatoes. Cook, uncovered, over low heat, stirring occasionally, for about 1 hour, or until the sauce thickens enough to coat a spoon.

Serve with Jersey Sunday Meatballs (page 149), or use as a go-to basic sauce.

HERB PESTO

MAKES 1½ CUPS

In the early nineties, I had my first taste of pesto on pasta and I couldn't believe that four simple ingredients were able to give revolutionary depth of flavor. For me, throwing a bunch of fresh herbs in a blender is the best way to get a boatload of flavor into a dish quickly—and you don't even need to heat the stove. I know that traditional pesto is more than just an herb puree, but the idea of a full-on flavor infusion is the same, and it's fun to experiment with all sorts of herbs and flavor combinations. Any sort of soft-leaf herb, including delicate bitter greens like arugula, makes for a wonderful pesto.

2 fresh mint sprigs (½ cup leaves)

1 bunch fresh flat-leaf parsley (1 cup packed leaves)

1 bunch fresh basil (2 cups packed leaves)

3 medium garlic cloves, chopped

Zest and juice of 2 lemons

1 teaspoon kosher salt, plus more as needed

1 cup extra-virgin olive oil

PREP: PICK THE LEAVES FROM THE STEMS FOR ALL THE HERBS AND DISCARD THE STEMS • PEEL AND CHOP THE GARLIC • ZEST AND JUICE THE LEMONS

1. Combine all the ingredients except the oil in the bowl of a blender or food processor and blend, streaming in the olive oil, until just combined. Try not to overblend to the point of a smooth paste; I recommend keeping the pesto a little chunky for texture.

2. Taste and adjust the seasoning, adding more salt if desired.

---

* Sauce your fresh homemade pasta (see page 18) with this pesto, or add it as a brightening flavor to Toasted Quinoa Soup (page 140).

* Play with herbs according to what looks great at the market—use mint in the summer, or try sage with meats such as lamb, pork, or turkey. Or add a small handful of toasted nuts, such as walnuts, almonds, pecans, or the traditional pine nuts.

Oh, the bunch conundrum! Trying to gauge "bunches" for this book was grueling! For every grocery store that sells herb "bunches" in 1-ounce packages, another market sells a bunch that amounts to nothing short of a bouquet! One person's "half bunch" is another person's "3 bunches." Rather than measuring, think in ratios and flavors. Whichever herb you want to stand out the most should be the most plentiful in your pesto—then cut down from there.

SWEET AND SPICY CHILI OIL

MAKES ABOUT 2 CUPS

Back in the day when supertraditional French and Italian cuisines were getting muscled out by a younger generation of American regional chefs, these same chefs started to celebrate infused-oil combinations as sauces to create beautiful colors and flavors on plates of the Southwestern cuisine that became popular in the early nineties. These days, flavored oils are ubiquitous. Entire stores are devoted to selling only infused oils. While not all oil infusions are successful—blueberry oil, I'm looking at you—some are here to stay, and that's as it should be.

This chili oil, a subtle combination of sweet and spicy peppers, is an absolute workhorse. It can be used for many types of cuisines and will punch up almost any dish that requires an injection of just-right spice. Eggs, pizza, fish, pasta, stir-fries—you name it, I've put chili oil on it!

1 Fresno chile or jalapeño pepper, chopped

2 red bell peppers, chopped

1 cup plus 2 tablespoons olive oil

2 tablespoons tomato paste

2 tablespoons chili powder

1 teaspoon dry mustard powder

1 tablespoon whole coriander seeds

1 tablespoon whole cumin seeds

2 tablespoons paprika

1 cup canola oil

PREP: WASH AND CHOP ALL THE PEPPERS

1. In a small saucepan over medium heat, sauté the Fresno and bell peppers in 2 tablespoons of the olive oil for 3 to 5 minutes, or until fragrant and softened. Add the tomato paste and cook for 1 minute more.

2. Add the remaining 1 cup olive oil and the remaining ingredients and cook over very low heat for 15 minutes, then remove the pan from the heat and let it steep for 1 hour.

3. Strain the oil through a fine-mesh strainer, reserving the liquid and discarding the solids.

* Use this chili oil for the Scallop "Ceviche" recipe (page 244) or drizzled on top of the Pulled Pork Sandwiches (page 159).

* This flavored oil will last for a long time in a tightly sealed jar in your refrigerator.

GREEN OLIVE RELISH

MAKES 2 CUPS

Cerignola olives are ideal for this recipe. Big and green and flavorful, they leave a lasting impression when you need to dress up a dish. But they can be hard to find, and if your local market doesn't carry them, don't let it stop you from trying this recipe! Instead, use the largest green olives you can find and work away!

¼ cup julienned preserved lemon

1 cup julienned green olives, in their juice

2 garlic cloves, sliced

¼ cup lemon juice (from 2 lemons)

1 cup extra-virgin olive oil

PREP: JULIENNE THE PRESERVED LEMON AND THE OLIVES • RESERVE 2 TABLESPOONS OF THE OLIVE JUICE • PEEL AND SLICE THE GARLIC • JUICE THE LEMONS

1. Combine all the ingredients in a large bowl. Let the ingredients mingle together for at least 1 hour before serving to allow the flavors to blend well.

*** Use this relish as a cold condiment on sandwiches or mixed into a pasta salad, or you could warm it slightly to use as a sauce on top of fish, chicken, or pork. It's particularly delicious on top of the Seared Scallops (page 221).**

Preserved Lemons

Preserved lemons are widely available in most grocery stores, or try this method for prepared lemon peel: Julienne the zest of 2 lemons and blanch the zest in a simple syrup made of 1 cup water, 1/2 cup sugar, and 1 tablespoon kosher salt. Boil until the zest is tender, drain, and use as preserved lemon or refrigerate for later use.

FRESH TOMATO SAUCE

MAKES 4 CUPS

This sauce is proof that an uncomplicated dish doesn't have to be boring or bland. A complete celebration of fresh, in-season tomatoes, it's great on lamb burgers (see page 122), or try it drizzled over a hearty salad or a piece of grilled fish. When tomatoes are in season, this sauce will be on the table every night!

3 cups chopped fresh plum tomatoes

1 garlic clove

½ cup olive oil

½ cup canola oil

1 teaspoon kosher salt

PREP: WASH, CORE, AND CHOP THE TOMATOES

1. Place the tomatoes and garlic in the bowl of a blender or food processor. Blend on low until the ingredients are finely chopped.
2. Stream both oils into the running blender or food processor. You'll see the color of the sauce gradually change from a deep red to almost orange. This is perfect—it means that the oil is emulsifying into the sauce.
3. Once the oil has been completely added, turn the blender up to high speed and add the salt. Pulse until the sauce is completely smooth.

*** Store this sauce in the fridge to have on hand for easy dinners, but keep in mind that it might separate, so just gently warm over low heat and then rewhisk or zap it in the blender again before serving.**

EASY COMPOUND LEMON-PEPPER BUTTER

MAKES 2 CUPS

Compound butters take me straight back to my earliest cooking days in culinary school. They seemed so upscale at the time—like something you'd only ever make in a restaurant. But what once seemed like a very traditional and fancy technique has become almost an essential go-to ingredient for whenever I need a flavor boost. The word *compound* alone can make anything seem more complicated than it is—but compound butter is simply butter mixed with herbs, zest, aromatics, or other seasonings. Think of butter as the carrier of whatever flavor you choose to mix in. I flavored this butter with the idea of using it on shellfish, but you could definitely slather a chicken with it just before roasting, or use it to finish off a basic risotto or to accompany the bread basket on your dinner table.

Compound butters can last a week or two tightly sealed in the fridge. Keep in mind that the butter becomes more perishable with the addition of fresh herbs.

1 tablespoon fresh oregano leaves

2 large shallots, halved

1 Fresno chile, halved

1 garlic clove

3 sticks (1½ cups) unsalted butter, at room temperature

2 teaspoons kosher salt

Zest and juice of 2 lemons

PREP: LEAVE THE BUTTER OUT FOR A COUPLE OF HOURS TO SOFTEN • PICK THE OREGANO LEAVES • HALVE AND PEEL THE SHALLOTS • HALVE AND SEED THE PEPPER • PEEL THE GARLIC • ZEST AND JUICE THE LEMONS

1. Combine the oregano, shallots, chile, and garlic in the bowl of a food processor or powerful blender. Puree until finely minced.

2. Add the butter and salt to the bowl of the food processor and pulse to incorporate. Using a spatula or wooden spoon, scrape down the sides of the processor bowl, making sure all the seasonings are brought from the bottom to the top. Blend on full speed until fully mixed, then add the lemon zest and juice and blend again until smooth.

3. Transfer the compound butter to a bowl, making sure to scrape all of the herbs and seasonings into the bowl. Set aside in a cool place if using right away, but refrigerate for longer storage.

* **This compound butter loves roasted lobster (see page 213).**
* **You can substitute jalapeño pepper, bell peppers, poblano peppers, or really any pepper for the Fresno chile.**

ALL-AROUND MUSTARD SAUCE

MAKES 2 CUPS

I have a hard time not eating this sauce with a spoon. I promise that once you make it, you'll be so glad to have it as part of your repertoire that you'll want to have it on hand all the time. I think of this as mainly a chicken or fish sauce, but it would be great with pork as well, and I wouldn't discount it for slathering on a corned beef sandwich, either! It's especially nice because rather than relying on mayo, it's cream based, which feels a little more elegant. It's truly an all-arounder!

5 shallots, thinly sliced

½ cup white wine

3 cups heavy cream

½ cup Dijon mustard

¼ cup grainy mustard

¼ teaspoon kosher salt

PREP: PEEL AND THINLY SLICE THE SHALLOTS

1. In a small saucepan over low heat, simmer the shallots in the wine until the liquid has cooked off, 4 to 5 minutes.
2. Add the cream and simmer over medium-low heat, whisking occasionally, until the liquid has reduced by half. Leave the whisk in the pot to keep the cream from boiling over.
3. Pour the mixture through a fine-mesh strainer into a bowl. Return the smooth cream to the saucepan, discarding the shallots. Add both mustards and whisk until smooth. Season with the salt.
4. Simmer over low heat for 5 minutes before serving or place in a tightly sealed jar in the refrigerator for use within 24 to 48 hours. To reheat, gently warm over low heat while stirring.

*** Serve this with pan-seared trout (see page 144), Corned Beef and Cabbage (page 174), or Poarched Arctic Char (page 229).**

GRAPEFRUIT GASTRIQUE

MAKES 1½ CUPS

A gastrique is a caramelized reduction of vinegar and sugar that is then finished with some sort of juice or stock. Gastriques are a chef's dream because they exhibit all the flavor balance we constantly strive for—in this case, sweet and sour. I always say that one big difference between home cooks and pro chefs is that pro chefs do not view a dish as complete without the addition of a sauce, which usually provides the balance and unity that dishes need. We often leave them off the menu at home, possibly because sauces might seem difficult or time-consuming or we don't want to dirty another pan. But here's your way in! Try this easy gastrique over fish, as a fancy citrus replacement for sliced lemons.

1 cup apple cider vinegar

¼ cup sugar

1½ cups ruby red grapefruit juice (from about 2 grapefruits)

PREP: JUICE THE GRAPEFRUITS

1. In a small saucepan over medium heat, whisk together the vinegar and sugar. Cook until the liquid has reduced to the consistency of caramel and can coat the back of a spoon, 8 to 10 minutes.
2. Whisk in the grapefruit juice and cook until the liquid has reduced by half, 8 to 10 minutes more.

* **It's important to use ruby red grapefruits here, as their naturally sweet undertones balance the acidic, tart flavor that dominates grapefruit. While fresh juice really sings in this recipe, if you can't find fresh ruby red grapefruits, use a good-quality ruby red grapefruit juice instead—one with no added sugar.**
* **Try orange juice instead of grapefruit for a twist.**

MALT VINEGAR AIOLI

MAKES 2 CUPS

I was first introduced to the magical pairing of fried foods with malt vinegar on a trip to England, where they automatically present a bottle of malt vinegar along with your fish and chips. One bite had me instantly hooked on the combination of superacidic vinegar and deliciously oily, crispy fried foods. This aioli is the direct result of my wanting to re-create those flavors. I originally thought about using this aioli as a dipping sauce for fries, but it quickly became a workhorse—great for sandwiches, fried foods, roasted potatoes, dipping chips, and more. Anything rich and crispy and salty and starchy—which is basically anything fried!

4 egg yolks

2 teaspoons Dijon mustard

3 tablespoons malt vinegar

1 garlic clove, roughly chopped

1 teaspoon sugar

Juice of 1 lemon

2 cups canola oil

⅛ teaspoon kosher salt

A few shakes of Tabasco (optional)

PREP: SEPARATE THE EGGS AND DISCARD THE WHITES, OR RESERVE THEM FOR A LATER USE • PEEL AND COARSELY CHOP THE GARLIC • JUICE THE LEMON

1. In the bowl of a food processor, combine the egg yolks, mustard, vinegar, garlic, sugar, and lemon juice. Turn the processor on to blend.
2. When the garlic is finely minced and the ingredients are combined, with the machine still running, gradually add the canola oil in a steady stream.
3. When the oil is in and the aioli has thickened, season with salt and a few shakes of hot sauce.
4. Refrigerate until ready to use.

Add the oil slowly. You're trying to emulsify the oil and egg, and if you add the oil too quickly, the mixture will separate. In a professional kitchen, we'd call the sauce "broken."

* If you find yourself without a food processor or blender—which is always the case for me—just use a whisk. To make an easier job of the hand-mixing, a great pro tip is to place a dampened kitchen towel under your bowl so that it doesn't move as you vigorously whisk. This frees up your other hand to pour the oil as you whisk. Do this anytime you're making vinaigrette or a sauce that requires you to drizzle oil slowly for emulsification.

* Serve with French fries, potato chips for game day, or even as a special sauce to fancy up a weekday burger.

ROSEMARY ANCHOVY RUB

MAKES ½ CUP

This rub is a cinch and really packs a flavor punch. Don't be afraid of the anchovies—they get such a bad rap! Anchovies offer the subtle je ne sais quoi behind so many sauces and rubs. In my chef brain, I think of briny anchovies as another way to season—an added dimension of welcome flavor, not as an overwhelming fish flavor. I promise that you won't taste the anchovies here—you'll only savor the subtle flavor they leave in their wake. This rub is just asking to be slathered all over any cut of lamb or beef you have on hand—racks, legs, steaks, chops. Even chicken can stand up to it! Simply massage it into the meat and roast, grill, or sear.

¼ cup fresh rosemary leaves

½ cup fresh flat-leaf parsley leaves

5 garlic cloves, roughly chopped

2 anchovies in oil, roughly chopped

¼ cup canola oil

PREP: PICK THE LEAVES FROM THE ROSEMARY AND PARSLEY • ROUGHLY CHOP THE GARLIC AND ANCHOVIES

1. Place all the ingredients except the oil in the bowl of a food processor or blender.
2. With the machine running, stream in the oil to blend into a semismooth paste. Use a spatula to remove all the rub from the food processor. (If you aren't using it immediately, you can store it in a tightly sealed container in the refrigerator for a day or two.)

---

* **Use your best tools—your hands—to generously coat the meat. Since it is a rub, not a marinade, it stays on the meat and acts as a seasoning, so cook it right away as desired.**
* **To make this by hand, roughly smash the mixture in a mortar and pestle, or even hand-chop all the ingredients as fine as possible.**

CURRY GOLDEN RAISIN SAUCE

MAKES 3½ CUPS

I am not 100 percent sure where my adoration for Indian cuisine stems from, but I think it's a combination of two things: the influence of my older brother, who studied in India for a long time, and my admiration for the expertly balanced array of spice blends found throughout the regions of India. So after cooking Italian pretty exclusively for seven years, I went to work at an American regional restaurant, where I had more leeway to play with a whole world of spices and flavors that had been out of bounds. On my days off, I devoted a lot of time to Indian food, trying to learn how the spice blends are put together with such balanced flavor profiles, highlighting perfect amounts of warmth, sweetness, and spice. In the case of this sauce, the warm and nutty browned butter helps strike that balance.

1½ cups golden raisins

1 cup chicken stock

1 tablespoon Madras curry powder

¾ teaspoon ground turmeric

4 tablespoons (½ stick) unsalted butter

1. In a medium saucepan over medium heat, combine the raisins, stock, curry powder, turmeric, and 2 cups water. Bring to a simmer and cook, uncovered, for 20 minutes.

2. When the simmering is almost done, in a medium sauté pan, heat the butter over medium-low heat until it begins to brown and foam, 2 to 3 minutes (it should smell toasty—see tip).

3. Carefully transfer the brown butter to the raisin sauce base. Stir until the butter combines with the rest of the sauce, then turn off the heat. Serve immediately or store in a tightly sealed container in the refrigerator for 1 to 2 days. To reheat, place in a saucepan over low heat and whisk to revive. Add a little more butter if necessary.

* This is an Indian curry primer of sorts—a great starter sauce for cooks maybe just beginning to venture into the world of spice blends and Indian cuisine. If your usual weeknight meal rotation includes a dish that features chicken with a side of rice, try this sauce as an accompaniment to experiment with new flavors.

* "Browning" butter brings out its inherent nutty flavors. But beware! There's a fine line between browning and burning, and the change can happen quickly. If the butter turns black, it's gone too far and you need to start over with new butter.

SWEET SUMMER CORN SAUCE

MAKES 4 CUPS

This recipe does double duty for me. It began as a corn soup, and just before it got to its thickest point, I stopped it and turned it into a sauce. But just add a bit more veggie stock to thin it out and chill it in the fridge and you'll have a delicious chilled corn soup.

Corn is at its best and in season during the summer. If you have a hankering for some sweet corn sauce and there's no good sweet corn to be found, use the highest-quality frozen corn niblets you can find—frozen veggies are often picked at their ripest and will offer better flavor than a fresh-but-out-of-season alternative.

The turmeric in this recipe provides a beautiful, vibrant yellow color that screams summer corn, even when I'm using a bicolor or white corn.

1 small Spanish onion, diced

2 tablespoons olive oil

½ cup diced red bell pepper

¼ teaspoon cayenne pepper

5 ears of corn (about 4 cups corn kernels)

¼ teaspoon ground turmeric

1½ cups heavy cream

½ tablespoon kosher salt

PREP: PEEL AND DICE THE ONION • WASH, SEED, AND DICE THE BELL PEPPER • SHUCK THE EARS OF CORN AND CUT THE KERNELS FROM THE COB

1. In a large sauté pan over medium heat, sauté the onion in the olive oil for about 10 minutes, or until the edges begin to turn translucent.
2. Add the bell pepper and cayenne and sweat (cook over low heat, stirring frequently) for 5 minutes, or until the pepper has softened.
3. Add the corn, turmeric, 1 cup of the cream, and the salt. Stir and cook over low heat for another 20 minutes, making sure not to let it boil.
4. Remove the pan from the heat and let the mixture cool slightly. Working in two batches, transfer the mixture to the bowl of a food processor or blender, divide and add the remaining ½ cup cream, a ¼ cup to each batch, and puree until smooth.

5. Once each batch has been pureed, combine them both in a large bowl or container and stir to mix well.

6. Reheat the sauce over low heat before using.

---

* **To separate corn kernels from the cob without getting corn all over the kitchen floor, place a cup or juice glass upside down in the center of a wide, deep bowl. Using the cup as a pedestal, hold the corn upright on top of it. Use the tip of a sharp chef's knife or even a serrated bread knife to "saw" back and forth, working your way down the length of the cob, watching those corn niblets fall neatly into the bowl as you go.**

* **When using corn for chowders or veggie soups, simmer the naked cobs in the liquid to reinforce it. The cob holds a ton of corn flavor that will infuse into your chowder or soup.**

* **Use this sauce for Hearty Gnocchi (page 215) or Poached Arctic Char (page 229), or try it for an added flavor boost to blanched asparagus (see page 9) or even to liven up your boiled or baked potatoes.**

CHERMOULA

MAKES 1½ CUPS

This chermoula is sure to raise eyebrows at the dinner table—especially since your guests will probably smell it before they see it. Chermoula is a sauce brimming with flavor that's found in Moroccan and other North African cuisines. It will bring a touch of the exotic to your table without taking people too far out of their comfort zones. The finished chermoula should not resemble a smooth pesto—rather, it should be dotted with lots of textural elements that introduce the sauce's components. Bright strands of lemon zest, bits of garlic, the orange hue of the paprika, and the occasional whole parsley or cilantro leaf are what make this a chermoula rather than a spiced herb pesto.

- 1½ cups roughly chopped fresh cilantro leaves
- 1½ cups roughly chopped fresh parsley leaves
- 5 garlic cloves
- 2 tablespoons ground cumin
- 1 teaspoon hot paprika
- Zest of 2 lemons
- 1 cup canola oil

PREP: PICK THE CILANTRO AND PARSLEY LEAVES • PEEL THE GARLIC • ZEST THE LEMONS

1. Combine all the ingredients except the oil in the bowl of a blender or food processor. Blend, streaming in the oil, until just combined. Do not overblend to a paste—keep it a little chunky for texture.

* **In place of an electric appliance, use a mortar and pestle, or, since you're going for chunky here, even hand-chopping and then mixing the ingredients in a bowl with a wooden spoon would be fine. If you're up for the hand-chopping, this is a great recipe for practicing those knife skills!**

* **I love to slather this versatile sauce on grilled flank steaks or salmon, and it makes for a scrumptious spread on grilled flatbreads or pita.**

FIRST IMPRESSIONS

You never have a second chance to make a first impression—a cliché, but totally true when it comes to food. In the restaurant world, an executive chef might get lucky and the food critic might anonymously duck in for a meal a few times before actually putting out that review—but a lot of times, you get just one shot to impress. Which is why every course, every meal, every night, we have to consistently bring our A game.

Appetizers and hors d'oeuvres are the opening act of that performance; they get diners excited with anticipation for the more substantial courses that will follow. In fact, in French cuisine a tiny morsel of a bite is often offered to diners at the very beginning of a meal—the amuse-bouche. Loosely translated, the word means "entertain the mouth." I love this visual! I always picture taste buds dancing with amusement and excited anticipation of the rest of the meal.

Sure, appetizers and hors d'oeuvres stave off diners' hunger and allow the kitchen time to fire entrées, but more important, they set a level of expectation and excitement (or, as is sometimes unfortunately the case, dread) for the dishes that are yet to come. At home, starters are often forgotten altogether, or they're the standard go-to cheese and crackers platter. I'm all for cheese and crackers, but appetizers and hors d'oeuvres are a great chance to show off and get your guests buzzing about your food. They're also an opportunity to experiment with ingredients that would otherwise be too costly, such as crab, prime cuts of beef, shrimp, or duck, or intimidating foods, like flan and phyllo dough. But appetizers and hors d'oeuvres need not be elaborate and expensive in order to impress—just delicious. And it's amazing how a small change like serving a basic gazpacho in shot glasses or your grandmother's beautiful antique teacups can make your dinner party feel more impressive in an instant. So have fun with presentation and ingredients—and make those taste buds dance!

First Impressions

EGGPLANT CAPONATA

MAKES 4 TO 6 SERVINGS

When I traveled to Sicily, I must have eaten no fewer than ten versions of eggplant caponata, and I never got sick of it! I also learned about the agrodolce—or sweet and sour—flavor profile that's so predominant in this dish, and in lots of Sicilian cuisine. My version of caponata is really flexible—serve it with crostini as a make-ahead appetizer, or even as a side dish. The addition of the briny capers, anchovies, and acidic vinegar help cure the eggplant and other veggies, so this dish only gets better in a tightly sealed container in the fridge, where it will last for up to a week.

2 large Italian eggplants, peeled and cut into medium dice

2 tablespoons kosher salt

5 tablespoons extra-virgin olive oil

1 red onion, thinly sliced

4 medium garlic cloves, thinly sliced

4 celery stalks, thinly sliced on an angle

2 anchovies, in oil

¼ cup tomato paste

1½ cups red wine vinegar

¼ cup sugar

½ cup capers, in brine

PREP: PEEL AND DICE THE EGGPLANTS • PEEL AND SLICE THE ONION • PEEL AND SLICE THE GARLIC • SLICE THE CELERY

1. In a large bowl, toss the eggplant with the salt. Transfer the eggplant to a colander to drain for 2 hours. In order to facilitate the draining, top the eggplant with a heavy weight, such as a dinner plate topped with full cans.

2. Heat 3 tablespoons of the olive oil over medium heat in a large sauté pan. Add the onion and sauté until translucent, 4 to 5 minutes. Add the garlic and celery and sauté for 5 minutes more, or until the garlic softens but does not brown. Add the anchovies and cook for 1 minute.

{ CONTINUED }

3. Add the tomato paste and stir to thoroughly combine. Cook for 2 minutes, or until the paste turns a deep red, almost brown, and starts to stick to the pan. Add the vinegar and sugar and stir until the mixture thickens, 3 to 4 minutes. Turn off the heat.

4. In another large sauté pan, heat the remaining 2 tablespoons olive oil over high heat until smoking. Add the eggplant and carefully toss it in the oil, letting it sear before stirring. Turn the heat down to medium and cook for 8 to 10 minutes, or until the eggplant is translucent and soft.

5. Transfer the eggplant to the caponata mixture and cook over low heat for 3 minutes, until the flavors combine. Add the capers and their brine and stir to incorporate.

6. Serve warm or at room temperature accompanied by toast points or crostini.

---

* **If you find some really beautiful different varieties of eggplant at your local farmers' market or store, feel free to sub them in. Look for rosa bianco, graffiti, or even white eggplant.**

* **When preparing eggplant, the "salt and drain" technique is necessary even though it's a little time-consuming. Without salting, the eggplant will act as a sponge and absorb all the oil, resulting in a very greasy eggplant dish.**

* **If you hate anchovies, leave them out!**

* **Feel free to sub in chopped olives and their brine for the capers.**

GAZPACHO

MAKES 4 SERVINGS
(OR 16 TO 24 HORS D'OEUVRES SHOOTERS)

As a chef, I'm extremely discerning when it comes to the quality of the raw ingredients that I use to prepare a dish. It's fair to say that if the raw ingredients don't taste good, then the finished product will be subpar, too. But there are cases when a particularly forgiving preparation will help a dish overcome slightly disappointing or not perfectly seasonal raw ingredients—for example, a long, slow braise or methodical layering of a cooked soup.

This isn't one of those recipes. It's one of the few in this book where you really can't make an exception—you must make it during your area's peak tomato season. This soup is really a chilled uncooked puree, and it will only ever taste as good as the whole veggies that went into it. Happily, though, it's worth the wait.

2 pounds fresh plum tomatoes, cored and coarsely chopped

1 cup tomato juice

1 cup coarsely chopped peeled cucumber

½ cup coarsely chopped red onion

¼ cup coarsely chopped red bell pepper

1 garlic clove

¼ cup red wine vinegar

¼ cup extra-virgin olive oil

⅓ cup fresh cilantro leaves

1 teaspoon kosher salt

¼ teaspoon freshly cracked black pepper

PREP: CORE AND CHOP THE TOMATOES • PEEL AND CHOP THE CUCUMBER AND RED ONION • SEED AND CHOP THE BELL PEPPER • PEEL THE GARLIC • PICK THE CILANTRO LEAVES

1. Combine all the ingredients in the bowl of a food processor or blender. Blend until almost smooth, but keep it slightly chunky for texture.

2. Taste and adjust the seasoning as needed.

3. Refrigerate—the gazpacho should be served well chilled.

* Just as you want to make sure your raw ingredients are tasty to begin with here, try to use high-quality extra-virgin olive oil and red wine vinegar. The olive oil and vinegar will make this dish really sing—so if you have a special bottle of olive oil that you were saving for just the right occasion, this is the time to break it out!

BUTTERNUT SQUASH SOUP

MAKES 3 QUARTS OR 6 SERVINGS

I've never met anyone who doesn't like butternut squash soup. It's a crowd-pleaser and so easy to make your own. It's colorful, it can be made ahead, and it's incredibly versatile—try adding coconut milk, finishing with toasted, chopped pecans, and/or cinnamon; serve it hot, serve it cold. And this vegetarian soup can easily be made vegan by omitting the cream.

3 tablespoons olive oil

2 Spanish onions, diced

3 garlic cloves, thinly sliced

2 teaspoons kosher salt

2 green apples, unpeeled, cored and diced

1 tablespoon Madras curry powder

⅛ teaspoon cayenne pepper

4 pounds butternut squash (about 2 large squashes), peeled and cubed

2 cups vegetable stock

1 cup heavy cream

PREP: PEEL AND DICE THE ONIONS • PEEL AND SLICE THE GARLIC • CORE AND DICE THE APPLES • PEEL AND CUBE THE BUTTERNUT SQUASH

The most important step in making soup is taking the time to properly build and layer flavors, so really give the onions and garlic adequate time to cook here.

Be careful—hot liquids can expand and explode in the blender or food processor, so be sure to cool the liquid, and don't fill the blender too full!

1. Heat the olive oil in a large soup pot over medium heat. Add the onions, garlic, and 1 teaspoon of the salt and sauté until the onions are translucent and sweaty, achieving no color, about 10 minutes.
2. Add the apples, curry powder, and cayenne and cook for 2 to 3 minutes to extract the apple flavor and bloom the spices.
3. Add the squash and stock, season with the remaining 1 teaspoon salt, and stir to combine. Bring to a boil, turn down the heat to maintain a low simmer, and cook, uncovered, for 30 to 45 minutes, or until the squash is fork-tender.
4. Add the cream, stir, and cook for 2 minutes more.
5. Remove from the heat and let the soup cool until you can safely transfer it to a blender or food processor, working in batches as needed.
6. Return the pureed soup to the pot to reheat, then serve, or transfer to containers, cool, seal tightly, and store in the fridge or freezer.

* In pro kitchens, everything sweats—not just the chefs, but the vegetables, too! "Sweating" is kitchen speak for cooking vegetables and aromatics in fat over low to medium heat to extract their flavor without achieving color. Be sure to season the vegetables and aromatics first, because the salt draws out the juices you need for sweating to happen.

MIXED MARINATED OLIVES

MAKES 2 CUPS

Every time I'm expecting guests, I head straight to the store and buy olives, booze, and chips—in that order. Mixed marinated olives are the perfect accompaniment to cocktails, wine, or beer because they're salty and rich. Here, I've combined four types of olives—although I've never met an olive I didn't like, so I'd use any type I had on hand. Also, right before my guests arrive, I make sure to "taste" an olive and purposefully leave the pit in a small bowl nearby, so everyone knows it's okay to follow suit. As an olive lover, I know what it's like to end up with a fistful of olive pits in a crushed napkin at the end of a cocktail hour!

½ cup extra-virgin olive oil

¼ cup Sicilian green olives

¼ cup Kalamata olives

¼ cup Niçoise olives

¼ cup oil-cured Moroccan or Sicilian black olives

Peel of 1 orange

2 garlic cloves, peeled

1 fresh rosemary sprig

½ teaspoon chili flakes

PREP: PEEL THE ORANGE, TAKING CARE TO RETAIN AS LITTLE PITH (THE WHITE LAYER) AS POSSIBLE • PEEL THE GARLIC

1. In a small saucepan over low heat, gently warm the olive oil to about 200°F, 6 to 8 minutes.
2. Combine the olives in a large bowl or mason jar.
3. Add the orange peel, garlic, rosemary, and chili flakes (these are the aromatics) to the oil and stir. Remove the pan from the heat and let the marinade cool to room temperature.
4. Pour the cooled marinade over the olives, cover, and marinate overnight at room temperature before serving.

* *Aromatics* are the flavoring ingredients that are added to a dish, such as garlic, shallots, herbs, citrus, lemongrass, and spices. To put your own mark on a recipe, play with the aromatics and make appropriate substitutions—herb for herb, citrus for citrus, spice for spice. With these olives, try thyme instead of rosemary or Meyer lemon for the orange.

SHRIMP COCKTAIL WITH HOMEMADE SAUCE

MAKES 2 CUPS

Who doesn't love shrimp cocktail? It always scores major fancy points but couldn't be easier to make—even when you concoct your own cocktail sauce. The cardinal sin of shrimp cocktail is serving mealy, overcooked shrimp; cooking them with the peel on will help prevent them from overcooking. Also, leave enough time to chill the shrimp well—it's important to serve them to your guests ice cold!

1 recipe poaching liquid (see the poaching liquid for arctic char, page 229)

1 pound whole shrimp, tail and peel on

2 cups ketchup

1½ teaspoons freshly cracked black pepper

¼ cup lemon juice (from about 2 lemons)

2 tablespoons prepared or grated fresh horseradish

PREP: PREPARE THE POACHING LIQUID • JUICE THE LEMONS • PEEL AND GRATE THE HORSERADISH, IF USING FRESH

1. Bring the poaching liquid to a gentle simmer in a wide, shallow pan over low heat. Add the shrimp and poach them for 10 minutes, or until they turn pink. Drain the shrimp and let them cool until they're cool enough to handle.
2. Peel the shrimp, leaving the tails on.
3. Look for the dark "vein" that runs the length of the shrimp's back. In order to remove it without destroying the shrimp, I recommend laying the shrimp on its side and carefully running a sharp paring knife down its back to make a shallow cut. Use the tip of the knife to extract the exposed vein.
4. Refrigerate the shrimp until you're about to serve them.

5. Meanwhile, in a medium bowl, whisk together the ketchup, pepper, lemon juice, and horseradish to make the cocktail sauce. Taste the sauce and season with more horseradish if you want to add extra kick. Refrigerate.

6. Serve both the shrimp and cocktail sauce very cold.

*** Try this poaching liquid for other types of seafood, such as trout, halibut, or even octopus!**

FAST GUACAMOLE

MAKES 1½ CUPS

Texture is just as important as flavor, and my "crunch" addiction proves that. Chips and guacamole are far and away one of my most-loved snacks, and once I start, I can't be stopped until either the chips or the guac are completely spent. I adore this guacamole recipe because it's a one-bowl wonder, with very few ingredients. The result is a creamy dip that's packed with flavor and can stand up to any chip—or margarita, for that matter.

- 4 ripe avocados
- ¼ cup lime juice (from 2 to 3 limes)
- ¼ cup diced red onion
- ¼ cup chopped fresh cilantro
- ¼ teaspoon kosher salt
- ¼ teaspoon cayenne pepper

PREP: JUICE THE LIMES • DICE THE ONION • CHOP THE CILANTRO

1. Cut the avocados in half lengthwise, around the pit. Cut each half in half again and throw out the pits. Either peel the skin away from the flesh or use a large spoon to scoop it out. Dice the avocado flesh and transfer it to a large bowl.
2. Add the remaining ingredients and smash the mixture together with a potato masher, heavy wire whisk, or fork. Once the ingredients have broken down, ditch the masher and stir with a spoon.
3. Taste and adjust the seasoning as you like it. Add more cayenne, lime, or cilantro—customize it to your own taste!

---

* **If your avocados are hard, speed up the ripening process by throwing them in a paper bag for a day or two. For same-day use, sorry, you'll have to buy them already ripe. A ripe avocado is soft at the stem end if you press it gently with your thumb.**
* **Guacamole is best served immediately, but if you're worried it will brown before you serve it, keep one of the avocado pits in the bowl of prepared guac. This, and the lime juice, will help stave off browning for a while.**

CRABMEAT CROSTINI

MAKES 20 PIECES

As with champagne, I break out crabmeat only on special occasions. Jumbo lump crabmeat is definitely not cheap, but when you want to create the perfect bite that's sure to be a hit and impress your guests, turn to this recipe. Because crabmeat always seems so decadent and special, I crafted this appetizer so that the other ingredients don't overpower the wonderfully sweet flavor of the crab—they just highlight it!

CROSTINI

1 brioche loaf, cut into 2-inch rounds, triangles, or squares with a biscuit or cookie cutter or a serrated knife

6 tablespoons (¾ stick) unsalted butter

1 tablespoon Old Bay seasoning

CRAB SALAD

1 pound jumbo lump crabmeat, picked through for shells

2 tablespoons small-diced celery

1 bunch fresh chives, minced

⅓ cup Mustard Vinaigrette (page 24)

Fresh chervil sprigs, for garnish

PREP: CUT THE BRIOCHE INTO ROUNDS, TRIANGLES, OR SQUARES • PICK OVER THE CRABMEAT • DICE THE CELERY • MINCE THE CHIVES • MAKE THE MUSTARD VINAIGRETTE • PICK TINY CHERVIL SPRIGS

1. To make the crostini, preheat the oven to 350°F. Place the brioche rounds on a baking sheet.

2. In a small saucepan over low heat, melt the butter with the Old Bay seasoning.

3. Generously brush the seasoned melted butter onto each brioche round and toast in the oven until just lightly golden, which will take just a couple of minutes, so keep a watchful eye. Remove and set aside to cool.

4. To make the crab salad, in a large bowl, combine the crabmeat, celery, and chives. Add the vinaigrette and gently combine with clean hands or a spoon or spatula, taking care not to break up the chunks of crabmeat, until all the ingredients are nicely dressed. Refrigerate until ready to serve.

5. Just before serving, top the brioche rounds with the chilled crabmeat salad, garnish each with a sprig of chervil, and serve.

* If you can't find brioche, use any other type of thick-cut bread. Even really good-quality store-bought crackers will work in a pinch.

* This crostini technique is also a great foundation for other appetizers, such as Eggplant Caponata (page 63).

GOAT CHEESE FLAN

MAKES FOUR 4-OUNCE FLANS

In the professional cooking world, I'm always trying to experiment, to re-create classic dishes with personal touches that make them unique again. Flan is commonly found sweet and drenched in caramel, but it's possible to make a savory flan flavored with almost any cheese, veggie, or herb. I chose goat cheese for this flan because of its natural elegance and great flavor. I always feature a goat cheese on my cheese platters, so I figured, why not shake it up a little by serving a goat cheese flan with crackers instead?

Nonstick cooking spray

¾ cup heavy cream

3 large eggs

6 ounces soft goat cheese, crumbled

½ teaspoon freshly cracked black pepper

¼ teaspoon kosher salt

1. Preheat the oven to 350°F and make sure the oven rack is in the center position. Grease four 4-ounce ramekins with nonstick cooking spray and set them in a larger baking dish that's about the same height as the ramekins.

2. In a large bowl, whisk together the cream, eggs, cheese, pepper, and salt until the mixture is smooth.

3. Divide the flan mixture evenly among the ramekins.

4. Pull the oven rack forward and rest the baking dish on the center of it. Fill a large measuring cup or teakettle with hot tap water and carefully pour the hot water into the baking dish so that it surrounds the ramekins and comes about 1 inch up their sides, taking care not to splash water into the ramekins. This water bath will help the flans cook evenly.

{ CONTINUED }

5. Gently push the rack back into the oven so that the baking dish is in the center. Bake for 25 minutes, or until the flans are set but still slightly jiggly in the center. Let the flans cool to just warm before handling them.

6. Use a small offset spatula or the tip of a paring knife to loosen the sides of the flans, then flip them onto serving plates to unmold. (Or you can certainly eat them right out of the ramekins—the presentation is up to you!)

*** A water bath (or bain-marie) allows delicate custard- or cream-based dishes to cook evenly and gently, without direct heat. The hot water distributes heat evenly around the baking vessel while also adding steam, keeping everything moist. You'll find water baths used in recipes for cheesecake, baked custards, and even bread puddings.**

SPINACH-FETA PIES

MAKES 8 HAND PIES

At family gatherings when I was growing up, my mom often bought frozen spinach-feta pies and served them by the platter alongside the mini quiches and pigs in a blanket. They were always buttery, with a perfectly flaky crust and sumptuously soft center—no wonder everybody loved them. My fond memories of those frozen pies inspired me to create my own. This recipe might seem time-consuming and a little intimidating, but these pies actually benefit from time spent in the freezer, so they're perfect to have on hand when you have unexpected visitors or are planning a dinner party.

- 1 large Spanish onion, diced
- ½ cup plus 2 tablespoons (1¼ sticks) unsalted butter, melted
- ¼ teaspoon plus a pinch kosher salt
- 2½ pounds fresh spinach
- 2 cups crumbled feta cheese
- ½ cup cottage cheese
- 3 large eggs
- ⅛ teaspoon freshly cracked black pepper
- 1 (16-ounce) box frozen phyllo dough, defrosted

PREP: MELT THE BUTTER • DICE THE ONION • WASH THE SPINACH THOROUGHLY • BEAT 1 EGG TO MAKE AN EGG WASH • UNROLL THE PHYLLO ONTO A BAKING SHEET AND COVER IT WITH A LIGHTLY DAMP TOWEL

In my hand, a "pinch" of salt is roughly 1/8 teaspoon. Problem solved!

1. Preheat the oven to 350°F.
2. In a large sauté pan over medium-low heat, sweat the onion (cook over low heat, stirring frequently) in 2 tablespoons of the melted butter until translucent. Season with a pinch of salt.
3. Add the spinach and cook until wilted, 3 to 4 minutes. Turn off the heat and transfer the mixture to a colander to cool.
4. When the spinach is cool enough to handle, drain it well by pressing it against the sides of the colander with your hands. Once most of the

{ CONTINUED }

liquid has been released, squeeze handfuls of the spinach to make sure all the excess water is removed. Transfer the mixture to a large bowl.

5. Add the feta, cottage cheese, 2 eggs, the remaining ¼ teaspoon of the salt, and the pepper to the bowl. Use a wooden spoon or rubber spatula to mix well. Set aside.

6. Working with one sheet of phyllo at a time, place a phyllo sheet horizontally on a cutting board and brush with melted butter. Lay another sheet on top and brush it with butter. Do this until you have a stack of 8 sheets.

7. Cut the stacked sheets in half lengthwise, then cut each in half again lengthwise, to get 4 narrow strips. Cut each strip in half horizontally to get 8 equal rectangles.

8. Place 2 heaping tablespoons of filling at the top left corner of one of the rectangles.

9. Paint the bottom and right sides of each rectangle with melted butter (like an inverted L). Starting with the top left corner of filling, fold the rectangle as you would a flag to create a triangle, pressing to seal after each fold. Fold any excess phyllo onto the triangle to seal it completely. Fill and fold the rest of the rectangles, to make 8 triangular pies. (See tip for make-ahead instructions.)

10. Brush the top of each pie with egg wash to seal and give a golden brown color when baking.

11. Transfer the pies to a baking sheet and bake for 20 to 25 minutes, or until golden brown.

*** If you are making these pies ahead of time, place them in one even layer on a baking sheet and freeze them completely, then consolidate them in a freezer bag or Tupperware container to save space. When baking the frozen pies, allow 10 additional minutes of baking time.**

MORE THAN A SALAD

Let's face it. *Salad* does not always get the taste buds going in the same way that *steak* or *burger* does. But just as with any other dish, as a chef I think of it as so much more than uninspired greens in a bowl drowning in dressing. In fact, when I set out to make myself a salad at home, I don't even necessarily start with the idea of greens. I think about all the elements in the same way I do for a composed dish—starch, protein, sauce, balance, texture—and then I scan my pantry and fridge and get inventive. I often call the result my "kitchen sink" salads—because I throw everything into them.

It's easy to get stuck in the rut of the same old typical salad ingredients, such as shredded carrots, tomatoes, and cucumbers. But salads are an opportunity for creativity. What if you forgo the usual ingredients and roast beets instead? Or, as in panzanella, how about making the croutons a central component, not just a stale afterthought? To make a salad eat more like a well-rounded meal with protein, start to think beyond just grilled chicken. How about lobster or bacon or quinoa? In France, herb salads are ubiquitous. Chopped tarragon, parsley, dill, and basil are always welcome additions that infuse flavor and depth into even the plainest of green salads.

Dressing the salad is the final step in building a successful one. Making your own vinaigrettes and dressings really pays off in the flavor department, and it couldn't be easier; you get to control your ingredients at a fraction of the cost. I never use any of the gummy, salty, sugary concoctions you find on the salad dressing shelves in the supermarket, because dressing is just so easy and satisfying to make. It can be as simple as olive oil and lemon juice or vinegar! (Check out pages 23 to 26 for other options.)

Correctly dressing a salad is a practiced skill, too. Too much or too little can make or break an otherwise perfectly conceived salad. In the kitchens of good restaurants, in order to make sure that salads get just the right amount of dressing, each salad is individually dressed and tossed in a mixing bowl before it's plated. In homes, salad dressings are often viewed as condiments, but chefs see vinaigrettes as the cold sauces of a dish. Just as I would never give guests a squeeze bottle of hollandaise to dress their own eggs Benedict, I'd never serve a bottle of salad dressing. The right amount of dressing is part of the art of making a delicious salad, and it's the chef's job to dress the salad correctly before it hits the table. In the restaurant, we use food handler gloves to gently toss a salad in its dressing, but at home, I feel that mixing the salad with my hands really helps to incorporate the vinaigrette throughout the greens while saving the greens from bruising. Your end result will be a salad that feels like a pro chef had her hands in there!

I include some of my favorite salads in this chapter, but the possibilities are endless if you mix and match flavors and ingredients—in fact, I think it would be possible never to make the same salad twice. Also, never underestimate the power of texture in a salad; the simple addition of common pantry items like toasted nuts and seeds, homemade croutons made from whatever bread you have on hand, and toothsome farro, couscous, or brown rice all add a textural profile that will make for a more interesting and wholesome salad. A salad to get excited about.

More Than a Salad

Start with less dressing than you think you need and add as you go. Once that dressing is on the salad, there's no removing it!

CAESAR SALAD WITH HOMEMADE BUTTER CROUTONS

MAKES 4 SERVINGS

Caesar salad often brings to mind the stereotypical tableside preparation where a waiter expertly employs the wide base of a wooden bowl to blend the classic ingredients of a Caesar dressing. When the crisp romaine is added, the perfect amount of dressing makes it onto every single leaf in the salad. Great Caesar salads are balanced—not overly gloppy or cheesy, but crisp and flavorful and creamy, with clear notes of citrus and brine from the anchovy. And let's not forget the buttery croutons that should enhance the salad, not bring it down by being a stale, sad afterthought. Caesar salads are everywhere these days—but it's hard to find a good one. Here's my version.

CROUTONS

1 cup 1-inch bread cubes

1 tablespoon butter, melted

½ cup grated Parmesan cheese, plus more for serving

SALAD

1 head romaine lettuce, washed, dried, and torn into rough pieces (4 cups, if using romaine hearts)

6 cracks black pepper

A dusting of grated Parmesan cheese

⅓ cup Caesar Dressing (recipe follows)

PREP: CUT THE BREAD INTO CUBES • MELT THE BUTTER • GRATE THE PARMESAN FOR THE CROUTONS AND THE SALAD • PREP THE ROMAINE • MAKE THE CAESAR DRESSING

1. To make the croutons, preheat the oven to 350°F and make sure the oven rack is in the center position.

2. Put the cubed bread in a small bowl. Pour the melted butter over the bread, add the grated Parmesan, and mix to coat the bread.

3. Transfer the coated bread cubes to a small baking sheet and bake for 10 to 12 minutes, or until the croutons are crispy and golden. Remove from the oven and set aside to cool.

{ CONTINUED }

4. To make the salad, in a large salad bowl, combine the romaine, pepper, Parmesan, a small amount of the Caesar dressing, and the croutons. Use your clean hands to toss well, coating the romaine evenly. Add more dressing if necessary.

5. Divide the salad evenly among four salad plates. Finish with more Parmesan just before serving.

CAESAR DRESSING

MAKES 2 CUPS

This dressing will last for twenty-four to forty-eight hours in a tightly sealed container in the fridge. Its shelf life is short because of the raw egg yolks.

3 egg yolks

2 tablespoons Dijon mustard

3 garlic cloves

5 anchovies

½ cup grated Parmesan cheese

1¼ cups canola oil

Juice of 2 lemons

PREP: SEPARATE THE EGGS • JUICE THE LEMONS

1. Combine the egg yolks, mustard, garlic, anchovies, and Parmesan in the bowl of a food processor or blender and process until smooth.

2. With the blender still running, slowly drizzle in the oil until it emulsifies and the dressing thickens.

3. While still blending, add the lemon juice and ¼ cup cold water to thin it out.

BEET SALAD WITH BEET VINAIGRETTE

MAKES 2 SERVINGS

This is a completely atypical beet salad. You see roasted beet salads on menus all the time, but here the salad features raw beets, which are so much sweeter, juicier, and crunchier than soft, earthy roasted beets. One of the joys of being a chef is turning on the creative juices to try to convert people with food aversions, and this beet salad gets supposed beet-haters every time. So give it a go, even if you think you're not a fan of beets.

½ cup pistachios, chopped and toasted

⅛ teaspoon sugar

⅛ teaspoon kosher salt

2 large beets, peeled and julienned, with ¼ cup trimmings (leftover after julienne) reserved to make the vinaigrette

¼ cup Beet Vinaigrette (recipe follows)

1 bunch watercress

1 cup (8 ounces) mascarpone cheese

PREP: CHOP AND TOAST THE PISTACHIOS • JULIENNE THE BEETS AND RESERVE THE TOPS • MAKE THE BEET VINAIGRETTE • RINSE AND DRY THE WATERCRESS

1. Preheat the oven to 325°F. Spread the pistachios on a rimmed baking sheet and sprinkle with the sugar and kosher salt. Toast for 3 to 4 minutes, or until lightly browned and fragrant. Set the baking sheet aside to cool.
2. In a large bowl, use a spoon or tongs to toss the beets with the pistachios and vinaigrette. Let the mixture sit for 5 minutes.
3. Add the greens and toss the salad again to coat the greens in the dressing.
4. Spread a layer of mascarpone cheese in the center of two salad plates.
5. Top with the beet salad.

{ CONTINUED }

BEET VINAIGRETTE

MAKES 2 CUPS

1 cup red wine vinegar

¼ cup sugar

1 cup reserved beet trimmings

3 shallots, thinly sliced

½ cup extra-virgin olive oil

Pinch of salt

¼ teaspoon freshly cracked black pepper

PREP: SLICE THE SHALLOTS

1. In a medium saucepan over medium heat, bring the vinegar, sugar, reserved beet trimmings, and shallots to a boil. Simmer until the sugar has dissolved, about 1 minute.
2. Remove from the heat, add the olive oil, and season with the salt and pepper. Stir and set aside, allowing the flavors to develop while you finish the salad.
3. Strain the vinaigrette just before using it. Transfer the rest to a tightly sealed container and save in the fridge for up to 2 weeks.

* ***Julienne*** **is a French cooking term for cutting a vegetable into thin matchsticks.**

* **In the restaurant I make this salad with robiolina cheese, a supersoft Italian cow's milk cheese—velvety and luxurious, similar to American cream cheese. It can be hard to find outside a really nice cheese shop, which is always a fun excursion. But when I want to make this salad at home, I usually make it the way I have here—with mascarpone cheese as a substitute.**

KALE AND FARRO SALAD WITH AGED GOAT CHEESE

MAKES 4 SERVINGS

Most green salads, once dressed, should be eaten right away because the dressing wilts the greens and the whole thing becomes soggy. With a base of hearty kale and even heartier farro, this salad actually benefits from sitting for up to two hours before you eat it. The kale becomes enjoyably toothsome when it loses its raw edge, and extra time allows the flavors to develop. In this case, add the goat cheese just before serving.

FARRO

½ cup uncooked farro

1½ cups water or vegetable stock

¼ teaspoon kosher salt

⅛ teaspoon freshly cracked black pepper

SALAD

1 small bunch kale

Juice of 1 lemon

1 garlic clove, thinly sliced

2 tablespoons extra-virgin olive oil

¼ cup shaved aged goat cheese

PREP: JUICE THE LEMON • PEEL AND SLICE THE GARLIC

1. To make the farro, in a medium saucepot, combine the farro with the water and bring to a simmer. Cover and cook for 20 to 30 minutes, or until the farro is tender.

2. Drain the farro in a colander and transfer it to a bowl. Season with the salt and pepper and set aside to cool.

3. To make the salad, remove and discard the woody stems of the kale. Finely chiffonade the kale leaves (see tip). You'll need about 2 cups kale chiffonade.

4. Place the kale in a large salad bowl. Add the lemon juice, garlic, and olive oil and use your clean hands or tongs to mix thoroughly.

5. Add the cooled farro and mix again, then taste and adjust the seasoning.

6. Evenly divide the salad among four salad plates, garnish with the goat cheese, and serve.

* To chiffonade means to cut leafy vegetables and herbs into ribbons. Just stack a few leaves, roll them into a cigar shape, and run your knife across the length of the roll in order to create thin strips.

* I was introduced to the ancient grain farro during my years in Italian restaurants, and it quickly became part of my home repertoire, too. You can substitute quinoa, short-grain brown rice, barley, Israeli couscous, or wheat berries if you like.

* You can use any variety of kale for this salad, or experiment with other hearty greens such as spinach or Swiss chard.

* I know that not everyone loves goat cheese, so feel free to use Parmesan or even feta here.

CUCUMBER, DILL, AND YOGURT SALAD

MAKES 4 TO 6 SERVINGS

I have to give all of the credit for this recipe to my Hungarian friend Vera, who taught me how to make this classic Hungarian salad. I adore dill and look for every chance to use it—soups, salads, and vinaigrettes. This salad gives me the rare opportunity to let dill be the star of the show. I've put my own twist on it by using Greek yogurt as the creamy component instead of the traditional sour cream.

1 tablespoon kosher salt, plus more as needed

1 teaspoon sugar

½ cup distilled white vinegar

1 tablespoon minced garlic

Pinch of cayenne pepper

1 small bunch fresh dill, chopped

1 cup plain Greek yogurt, preferably full fat

6 cucumbers, peeled and diced

PREP: PEEL AND MINCE THE GARLIC • CHOP THE DILL • PEEL AND DICE THE CUCUMBERS

1. In a large bowl, combine the 1 tablespoon of salt, the sugar, vinegar, garlic, and cayenne. Whisk until the sugar has dissolved.
2. Add the dill and yogurt and stir with a large spoon to incorporate. Add the cucumbers and use a large spoon to gently mix the cucumbers to coat them without breaking them up. Taste and season with more salt if necessary.
3. Refrigerate for 30 minutes before serving.

*** This is not a salad that you make a day ahead. From the moment the salt hits the cucumbers, they'll start releasing liquid, and when you leave it in the fridge overnight, you'll find the cucumbers swimming in water by the next day.**

ASPARAGUS SALAD WITH PARMESAN

MAKES 4 SERVINGS

This recipe simply celebrates the beautiful union of asparagus and Parmesan cheese. With the addition of tarragon, diced hard-boiled eggs, and my Mustard Vinaigrette, this dish is a riff on the classically French asparagus mimosa. The bright yellow yolks bounce off the vibrant asparagus and greens to create a salad that's perfect for brunch with friends, or as a side to a piece of grilled fish or chicken. You can play with the greens, but I like them with a little bit of a bite for this salad, since the asparagus has such a distinct flavor.

2 bunches green asparagus, trimmed, blanched (see page 9), and cut on an angle into 2-inch pieces

1 cup frisée, sliced endive, mizuna, or arugula

1 teaspoon chopped fresh tarragon

¼ pound Parmesan cheese, grated, or ¾ cup grated Parmesan

Kosher salt and freshly cracked black pepper

2 hard-boiled eggs

2 tablespoons Mustard Vinaigrette (page 24)

Small saucepan, cover eggs with cold water, cover, and bring to a boil, cook for 12 minutes. Drain, cool before peeling.

PREP: TRIM, BLANCH, AND CUT THE ASPARAGUS • PREP THE GREENS • CHOP THE TARRAGON • GRATE THE CHEESE • BOIL AND PEEL THE EGGS • MAKE THE MUSTARD VINAIGRETTE

Chopping hard-boiled eggs can give you a mishmash mess. Using your hands retains nice texture, and you'll get your hands messy mixing the salad anyway.

1. Combine the asparagus, greens, and tarragon in a large bowl. Add half of the grated Parmesan, the salt, and the pepper to the mix.
2. Use your clean hands to break the eggs into bite-size pieces over the bowl.
3. Add the vinaigrette and use your hands to mix the salad well.
4. Serve it on a platter or divide it among four plates. Top with the rest of the Parmesan.

* When making salads, ensure that your greens are really dry after washing them. If they're at all wet, the dressing will run right off the leaves rather than coating them, resulting in a limp, watered-down salad.

"ITALIAN" SALAD

MAKES 4 SERVINGS

I grew up in an area of New Jersey that's riddled with Italian American restaurants and pizzerias, and I love them all! While I enjoy unhinging my jaw to bite into an impossibly stacked Italian hero as much as the next gal, sometimes I want to delight in the flavors of oregano, garlic, and vinegar mixed with Italian cold cuts and cheeses without the bread. And that's how I stumbled upon this salad—which, by the way, definitely eats like a meal and will satisfy even the hungriest of appetites. I promise you won't miss the bread.

- 4 or 5 thick-cut Genoa salami slices, quartered
- ¼ pound provolone cheese, cut into ½-inch cubes
- 6 celery stalks, cut into ½-inch slices on an angle
- ¼ cup celery leaves
- ¼ cup pitted black olives, roughly chopped
- 1 garlic clove, thinly sliced
- ¾ cup Red Wine Vinaigrette (page 26)
- 2 cups roughly chopped escarole

PREP: CUT THE SALAMI AND DICE THE PROVOLONE • CUT THE CELERY • CHOP THE OLIVES • PEEL AND SLICE THE GARLIC • MAKE THE RED WINE VINAIGRETTE • CHOP THE ESCAROLE

1. In a large bowl, combine all the ingredients except for the escarole. Let the mixture sit for 10 minutes so that the flavors mingle and marinate.
2. Add the escarole and mix to coat it with the dressing.

* **Escarole is strong and mighty, so if you need to substitute, go for a crunchy, crispy, hearty green that can stand up to the strong flavors in this salad. Try endive, radicchio, iceberg, or romaine instead.**

* **Soppressata, prosciutto, or any of your favorite cured Italian meats can be added or subbed in, just as Asiago, Parmesan, Gouda, pecorino, or even mozzarella can be added or subbed for the provolone.**

CORN AND BLACK BEAN SALAD

MAKES 4 SERVINGS

Corn and black beans together always bring me back to the Southwest. My brother lives in Tucson, Arizona, and while I don't get to visit him as often as I'd like, whenever I head to the Southwest I always look forward to the food (and my brother, of course!). This salad is the model for "more than a salad," because it can work as a dip with tortilla chips or a star in your summer BBQ side salad lineup or a filling for vegetarian tacos. No matter how you shuck it, this corn salad is a winner!

1 tablespoon canola oil

5 ears corn, husked and kernels cut from the cobs

¼ teaspoon kosher salt

1 cup canned black beans, drained and rinsed

½ cup diced beefsteak tomato

2 tablespoons sliced scallions

¼ cup chopped fresh cilantro

¼ cup fresh lime juice (from 2 limes)

Pinch of cayenne pepper

½ cup grapeseed oil

PREP: CUT THE KERNELS FROM THE CORNCOBS • DRAIN AND RINSE THE BEANS • DICE THE TOMATO • SLICE THE SCALLIONS • CHOP THE CILANTRO • JUICE THE LIMES

1. Heat the canola oil in a large sauté pan over medium-low heat. Add the corn kernels and salt and sweat (cook over low heat, stirring frequently), until the corn is bright yellow, tender, and warmed through, about 5 minutes.
2. Transfer the corn to a large bowl and add the rest of the ingredients. Mix well to combine.
3. Allow the salad to sit at room temperature for a couple of hours before serving.

* In place of the raw tomatoes, use the oven-roasted tomatoes from page 12 for added flavor intensity.

* Use parsley instead of cilantro, and if you're really into spicy food, try this salad with some finely minced jalapeño or additional cayenne pepper.

* If you can't find fresh corn or it's not in season in your area, feel free to use high-quality frozen corn kernels—there's a wide variety available in most supermarkets now. Just be sure that the corn doesn't have any added ingredients, and thaw it before cooking.

AVOCADO AND BACON SALAD WITH JALAPEÑO–BACON FAT DRESSING

MAKES 4 SERVINGS

You need only look at the title of this recipe to know that this is the anti-salad. Basically, it's all my favorite savory items put together, uniting forces to create an almost sinful salad. This salad accidentally came together as a result of pure kitchen resourcefulness! I had a hankering for bacon in my salad, and I needed a vinaigrette to top it off, so I used the left-over bacon fat as the fat in the dressing, and it was just as delicious as you'd think it would be. The hearts of palm and lime juice provide the perfect acidic antidote to what has the potential to be an overly fatty mouthfeel, and the jalapeño and Dijon mustard cut right through the bacon and avocado with a nice amount of spice, providing necessary balance. When you make this salad to wow your friends, the bacon fat vinaigrette can be our little secret!

12 slices bacon, diced

3 garlic cloves, minced

½ small jalapeño, seeded and minced

½ cup lime juice (from 3 to 4 limes)

1 tablespoon Dijon mustard

¼ teaspoon kosher salt

¼ cup canola oil

1 romaine heart, quartered

½ cup canned hearts of palm, drained and cut into ½-inch disks

1 avocado, pitted, peeled, and quartered

PREP: DICE THE BACON • PEEL AND MINCE THE GARLIC • SEED AND MINCE THE JALAPEÑO • JUICE THE LIMES • QUARTER THE ROMAINE HEART • SLICE THE HEARTS OF PALM • PIT, PEEL, AND QUARTER THE AVOCADO

For helpful tips on working with avocados, see the guacamole recipe on page 74.

{ CONTINUED }

1. Place a large skillet over high heat. When the skillet is hot, add the bacon and sear for a minute, then turn down the heat to low to continue cooking and rendering the fat. Cook until the bacon is crisp but still tender and not so crispy that it crumbles.

2. Strain the bacon and the rendered fat through a fine-mesh strainer, separating the liquid fat from the meat and reserving both.

3. In a blender or food processor, combine the garlic, jalapeño, lime juice, mustard, and salt. Puree until liquefied and smooth.

4. In a measuring cup, combine the rendered bacon fat and the canola oil. With the blender or food processor running, slowly drizzle in the fat-oil mixture until the dressing is completely emulsified.

5. In a large bowl, combine the quartered romaine hearts, hearts of palm, bacon bits, and 2 tablespoons of the dressing. Use your clean hands to gently mix the salad, coating the romaine evenly with dressing.

6. Transfer to a large platter or distribute evenly among four plates. Top the salad with the avocado and drizzle with more vinaigrette, if necessary.

---

* **This bacon dressing is also great as a warm dressing on hearty greens like spinach or kale. Reserve it in a tightly sealed container in the refrigerator and gently warm by removing it from the fridge in advance to bring to room temp or by setting it in a hot water bath just before adding it to the greens.**

GRILLED ZUCCHINI AND TOMATO PANZANELLA SALAD

MAKES 4 SERVINGS

For roughly seven years, I cooked in Italian food restaurants. Much of the philosophy of Italian cuisine revolves around the use of simple, beautiful ingredients and using everything you have in your kitchen, even the day-old bread! One of my simple salad-eating pleasures is finding that one crouton at the bottom of the bowl that has absorbed a ton of dressing and, along with it, all of the flavors of the salad. Panzanella is a classic example of the ingenuity that can come from using what you have, and a celebration of the basics of Italian cuisine.

1 cup day-old bread cubes

½ bunch fresh mint, chopped

2 tablespoons olive oil, plus more for drizzling on the bread

3 large zucchini, trimmed and cut lengthwise into 5 or 6 long slices each

½ teaspoon kosher salt

¼ teaspoon freshly cracked black pepper

½ pint cherry tomatoes, halved

8 fresh basil leaves

1 cup Red Wine Vinaigrette (page 26)

PREP: CUBE THE BREAD • PICK AND CHOP THE MINT • TRIM AND SLICE THE ZUCCHINI • HALVE THE TOMATOES • PICK THE BASIL LEAVES • MAKE THE RED WINE VINAIGRETTE

1. Preheat the oven to 325°F. In a large bowl, toss the bread cubes with the chopped mint and a drizzle of olive oil. Spread the bread cubes in an even layer on a rimmed baking sheet and bake until just slightly golden, 8 to 10 minutes. Set aside to cool.

2. Heat a grill or grill pan over high heat.

3. Season the zucchini slices with the 2 tablespoons olive oil, the salt, and pepper. Lay as many zucchini slices flat on your grill as it will accommodate. When you lay them down, you should hear a sizzle,

{ CONTINUED }

which is how you'll know the grill is hot enough. Grill for 1 to 2 minutes, or until lightly seared, then use tongs to turn the zucchini over. Cook for 1 minute, then remove the zucchini and set aside to cool.

4. Toss the cherry tomatoes and croutons in a large bowl. Add the cooled zucchini slices and ¾ cup of the vinaigrette and toss lightly. Let the salad sit and marinate for about 5 minutes, or until the croutons just begin to soften.

Don't cut the basil too far in advance, as it will brown and wilt, losing its pizzazz.

5. Chiffonade the basil leaves.

6. Add the basil to the salad, gently mix, and taste. If you need to, add more of the vinaigrette before serving.

*** Traditionally, panzanella includes tomatoes, which makes it a perfect summer salad. But there are no rules here! You can riff on this classic to your heart's desire and play with the vegetables and herbs that are in season or at your market.**

LOBSTER SALAD

MAKES 2½ CUPS OR 2 SERVINGS

Anything "lobster" instantly ups the fancy ante in a dish. This salad may *seem* fancy, and it's sure to make any guest feel extra special, but it's only as hard as cooking the lobsters—which isn't very hard. Once you've extracted the cooked lobster meat, it's just a matter of mixing in the other salad components and serving it up.

- 2 (1½-pound) live lobsters
- 2 to 3 tablespoons olive oil
- ½ cup mayonnaise
- ⅛ teaspoon Old Bay seasoning
- Juice of ½ lemon
- ¼ teaspoon kosher salt
- ⅛ teaspoon freshly cracked black pepper
- ½ cup diced celery
- ¼ cup diced red bell pepper
- ¼ teaspoon minced fresh tarragon
- ¼ teaspoon minced fresh chives
- Romaine leaves, for serving

Use 3 fresh or frozen lobster tails if you can't find fresh whole lobsters.

PREP: SPLIT THE LOBSTERS • JUICE THE LEMON • DICE THE CELERY AND PEPPERS • MINCE THE HERBS • WASH AND SEPARATE THE ROMAINE LEAVES

1. Roast the lobsters using the recipe for Oven-Roasted Lobsters (page 213), omitting the butter and drizzling with the olive oil instead. Set the cooked lobsters aside to cool.
2. When the lobsters are cool enough to handle safely, remove the meat from the shells and set it aside. Discard the shells.
3. In a large bowl, combine the mayonnaise, Old Bay, lemon juice, salt, and black pepper. Use a whisk or fork to blend well. Add the diced celery, bell pepper, and herbs and use a spoon to toss together.
4. Gently dice the lobster meat and add it to the bowl. Use your clean hands or a wooden spoon to gently toss the salad, coating the lobster well with dressing but taking care not to break up the delicate meat.
5. Serve the lobster salad on a bed of crisp romaine leaves.

* This is basically the filling for a lobster roll, so feel free to break out the split-top hot dog rolls and turn this dainty salad into a height-of-summer treat.

* Cook up and dice a pound of shrimp as an alternative, or even include some diced, cooked shrimp with the lobster for a shellfish salad.

WHAT'S FOR DINNER?

It's the million-dollar question.

A big reason I can find cooking at home difficult is the wall of exhaustion I often run into on an average weeknight. Days off from the restaurant never seem to be real days off—they're equally busy. It never fails that the hunger comes on just as I walk through the door, when all I feel like doing is kicking up my feet and relaxing. And I know I'm not alone in this. Whether you're cooking for a family or just yourself, after a busy and tiring day, there's nothing worse than getting home and staring blankly into the fridge hoping for divine inspiration to strike. In my case, the path of least resistance often leads me straight to the stockpile of take-out menus in my kitchen drawer. But, while takeout may feel like the easiest option, it certainly isn't the most wallet-friendly, healthy, or delicious one.

While it's ideal to have a plan in place for dinner at home, it's not always a realistic scenario. So over time I've learned to keep my chef hat on at home and view the situation as a challenge, like being on *The Next Iron Chef* or *Chopped,* but with slightly less at stake. It's the art of cooking on the fly—using what you have on hand to create something delicious. And these impromptu dishes ultimately offer the most satisfaction, because I end up with a delicious meal that didn't take too long to prepare, and I get to feel resourceful and thrifty in the process!

The recipes in this chapter use many of the staples you probably already have on hand in your pantry, fridge, or freezer, and they don't take a whole lot of time to prepare. Grains such as quinoa and polenta can easily hold their own as stand-alone side dishes or find their way into your meals in lots of other ways. An arsenal of dried herbs and spices ensures that you're always prepared to make deeply flavorful dishes, helping you get creative with a host of veggies and proteins in no time. With an easy spice rub, a plain ol' chicken thigh becomes a Jamaican-spiced chicken thigh. A few fresh vegetables combine with the lentils in the pantry and a hearty, healthy dinner is quickly on the table. No fresh herbs on hand? Turn to dried spices and you don't need a store run to make a sauce or soup. My old fridge faithfuls are eggs, butter, a wedge of Parmesan cheese, a jar of prepared horseradish, and bacon. I open the refrigerator door and know there's a delicious meal in my future!

And, as I mentioned in the "Back to Basics" chapter (page 1), stock is vital to have on hand, and we're over feeling guilty if it's not homemade. Just try a bunch and see which ones you like the best, keeping in mind that you'll want to control the amount of salt—you can always add it later. Having a few boxes of chicken, vegetable, and beef stock on hand is truly a game changer in terms of the flavors and meals you can achieve quickly at home.

My favorite thing about the weeknight recipes in this chapter is that there's nothing to limit them to weeknights—they're all great for entertaining, too. They're crowd-pleasers and fast to prepare, which makes them fantastic for when you have last-minute guests and need a gussied-up meal in a pinch.

What's for Dinner?

"PORK ON PORK" CHOPS

MAKES 4 SERVINGS

While I was executive chef at The Harrison, it didn't take long for this dish to become a favorite of mine, as well as of my staff and many of my regulars. People were surprised that a female chef would decide to feature a massive pork chop on the menu, and then have the nerve to top it with crispy pancetta bits and finish it off with a bath of rendered pork fat! The staff and I used to call it "pork on pork crime," but there's no crime in eating this dish, and there's a method to my madness: the eye of the pork chop is quite lean, so I knew I needed to infuse some moisture. Hence the pancetta fat. It's a complete success every time—and it will be for you, too!

1 pound pancetta, cut into small dice

2 tablespoons fresh thyme leaves

1 tablespoon fresh rosemary leaves

3 garlic cloves

4 center-cut pork chops, each about 2½ inches thick

Kosher salt and freshly cracked black pepper

3 tablespoons canola oil

PREP: DICE THE PANCETTA • PICK THE THYME AND ROSEMARY LEAVES • PEEL THE GARLIC

1. Preheat the oven to 400°F.
2. In a food processor, combine the pancetta, thyme, rosemary, and garlic. Pulse until the mixture is finely ground. Set aside.
3. Make sure the pork chops are at room temperature, then liberally season them with salt and pepper on both sides.
4. Heat the canola oil in a large oven-safe skillet or grill pan over high heat. When the oil is hot, sear the pork chops for about 2 minutes on each side.

{ CONTINUED }

5. Stick the pan in the oven to finish cooking the pork, 5 to 6 minutes. Depending on your oven, of course, and the thickness of your chops, this should result in a medium to medium-well chop, still slightly pink in the middle. If you prefer a more well-done chop, add a minute or two to the cooking time.

6. While the pork chops are in the oven, heat a large sauté pan over high heat. Add the pancetta and herb mixture. Turn the heat down to low and continue to cook the pancetta, stirring continuously to break up any large chunks, until all the fat is rendered and the pancetta is crispy, 8 to 10 minutes.

7. Serve the pork chops topped with the crispy herbed pancetta and rendered fat. Serve while hot and bubbling!

---

* **No pancetta around the house? Feel free to substitute bacon.**

* **If you don't own a food processor, finely dice the pancetta, herbs, and garlic using a sharp chef's knife and some good ol' elbow grease.**

* ***Render* is fancy food talk for allowing the fat to slowly cook out of a meat, which allows the meat to crisp while keeping the fat from burning. You'll hear it most often used in reference to pork and duck fat.**

SPINACH, POTATO, AND RICOTTA EGG WHITE FRITTATA

MAKES ONE 10-INCH FRITTATA, TO SERVE 4 TO 6

My life is food-centric, and while I consider myself very lucky to be surrounded by amazing food so much of the time, I do need to remember the old adage "Everything in moderation." So when I have the occasion to cook for myself at home, I tend to seek out dishes that will give me a break from all the indulgent eating I get to do, and eggs are my go-to for a clean, lean, quick, and satisfying meal. Sometimes it's as simple as putting a fried egg on top of a veggie leftover that lurks in my fridge, but often I put together an omelet, or a frittata, which is even easier, with no need to fold or flip! If you can scramble an egg, you can make a frittata.

2 small Red Bliss potatoes

8 egg whites (reserve the yolks for Hearty Gnocchi, page 215)

½ teaspoon kosher salt

3 tablespoons extra-virgin olive oil

1½ cups baby spinach

2 scallions, sliced

½ cup ricotta cheese

⅛ teaspoon freshly cracked black pepper

PREP: SCRUB AND WASH THE POTATOES • SEPARATE THE EGGS, RETAINING THE WHITES • PREP THE SPINACH • SLICE THE SCALLIONS

1. In a small saucepan over high heat, cook the potatoes in boiling water until tender, about 20 minutes. Drain the potatoes, let them cool, and cut them into 1-inch dice.

2. Preheat the oven to 350°F and make sure the oven rack is in the center position.

3. In a small bowl, combine the egg whites and ¼ teaspoon of the salt. Use a whisk or a fork to break up the egg whites and whisk until frothy.

{ CONTINUED }

4. Heat the olive oil in a 10-inch oven-safe skillet over medium heat. Add the egg whites, then immediately sprinkle in the potatoes, spinach, and scallions, spreading them evenly over the eggs. Evenly distribute dollops of the ricotta cheese all over the top of the frittata. Season with the remaining ¼ teaspoon salt and the pepper.

5. Bake for 8 to 10 minutes, or until the egg whites have just set and the edges begin to turn golden.

6. Run a rubber spatula around the edge of the frittata to make sure it releases fully from the sides of the pan. Tilt the pan slightly and coax the frittata out with the rubber spatula, carefully sliding it out of the pan and onto a large plate.

7. Cut into wedges and serve.

*** You can use almost any vegetable here in place of the spinach: kale, chard, arugula, escarole, broccoli rabe, asparagus, peas, cauliflower—go for it!**

*** The cheese is just as interchangeable—it doesn't even need to be a soft cheese.**

LAMB BURGERS WITH FRESH MINT YOGURT

MAKES 4 SERVINGS

Since I'm constantly tasting and munching on food at my restaurant, I rarely sit to eat an actual whole, balanced meal while at work. So, I'm always looking for ways to eat a little more consciously when I cook at home. This dish is a favorite of mine because it is packed with flavor and low on carbs, plus the quinoa adds nutrients and lots of fiber. And, while nutritional value is always important, these burgers also happen to be delicious, which is what it's all about, right?

1 cup uncooked quinoa

Kosher salt

1 pound ground lamb

1 large egg

1 small Spanish onion, diced

1 garlic clove, minced

2 teaspoons ground cumin

Pinch of cayenne pepper

2 tablespoons canola oil

2 tablespoons chopped fresh mint

1 cup plain Greek yogurt

PREP: DICE THE ONION • PEEL AND MINCE THE GARLIC • CHOP THE MINT LEAVES

1. Place the quinoa in a large fine-mesh strainer and rinse with cold water. Transfer the quinoa to a small saucepan and cover with 2 cups cold water. Bring the water to a boil over high heat, then turn down the heat to maintain a low simmer, season with a generous pinch of salt, and cook, covered, for 15 to 20 minutes, or according to the package instructions.

2. Remove the quinoa from the heat, fluff it with a fork, and transfer it to a large bowl to cool.

3. Add the lamb, egg, onion, garlic, spices, and 2 teaspoons salt to the cooled quinoa. Use clean hands or a wooden spoon to mix thoroughly.

4. Divide the mixture into four equal portions and form each into a ball, as you would a meatball. Place the balls on a large plate or baking sheet and gently use the heel of your hand to flatten them into thick patties.

5. Place a large nonstick sauté pan over high heat and add the canola oil. Let the oil heat for 1 minute, then add the patties to the hot pan. Sear for a couple of minutes on each side.

6. Cover with a lid or foil and turn down the heat to medium. Cook for another 10 to 12 minutes, turning once halfway through.

7. Meanwhile, in a small bowl, combine the mint and yogurt and season with salt.

8. Top the lamb burgers with a dollop of the mint yogurt and serve.

* **The lamb burgers can be served over your favorite salad or on a fresh bun, or in a pita with sliced onion and tomato, or try them over Fresh Tomato Sauce (page 43).**

"LUSTY" LEMON CHICKEN

MAKES 6 TO 8 SERVINGS

Chicken and lemon are always a match made in food heaven. The wonderful acidity of the lemon juice pairing with the fat of the chicken never fails to put a smile on my face. Over the years, I've cooked and eaten many versions of lemon chicken, and I think this one is a balance of perfect simplicity and mountains of flavor. It gained the name "lusty" when I made it for a deciding round of *The Next Iron Chef.* The judges called it one of the best chicken dishes they'd ever had! Not bad for the humble chicken and lemon.

2 (3-pound) free-range chickens

4 carrots, peeled and cut into large chunks

2 celery stalks, cut into large chunks on an angle

1 onion, peeled and cut into 8 wedges

4 garlic cloves, peeled

1 bunch fresh thyme

Kosher salt

Freshly cracked black pepper

½ cup (1 stick) butter, at room temperature

4 cups Chicken Stock (page 27) or store-bought sodium-free chicken stock

1 (4-ounce) Parmesan rind (the rind works best here, but you can use a chunk of the cheese if necessary)

2 lemons, halved

Buy whole chunks of Parmesan so you can freeze the rind and use it for soups.

PREP: LEAVE THE BUTTER OUT TO SOFTEN • PEEL AND CHOP THE CARROTS • CHOP THE CELERY • PEEL AND CUT THE ONION • PEEL THE GARLIC • HALVE THE LEMONS

1. Preheat the oven to 450°F.

2. Place one of the chickens breast side up on a poultry-specific cutting board and remove the thighs and drumsticks, then separate the thighs from the drumsticks. Place the thighs and drumsticks on a small baking sheet and refrigerate. Cut the wings off at the first joint and discard.

3. Flip the chicken over, cut out the backbone with kitchen shears or a sharp chef's knife, and discard it (or save it for stock or soup).

{ CONTINUED }

4. Flip the chicken over again and cut it down the middle between the breasts, breaking the breastbone and separating it into two pieces.

5. Repeat to cut up the second chicken.

6. In a roasting pan that will fit all four chicken breasts, combine the carrots, celery, onion, garlic, and thyme. Place the four breasts skin side up on top of the vegetables. Season the skin well with salt and pepper.

7. Use your fingers to create pockets between the skin and meat and distribute the butter evenly under the skin, pushing it into every nook and cranny.

8. Roast the chicken for 15 minutes. After 10 minutes of cooking, season the thighs and drumsticks liberally with salt and pepper. Place them in the same pan as the breasts and back into the oven for the remaining 5 minutes.

9. Turn the oven temperature down to 375°F and cook the chicken for 20 minutes.

10. Meanwhile, make a Parmesan broth: In a small saucepan over medium heat, bring the chicken stock and cheese rind to a simmer. Season with ¼ teaspoon of the salt and keep warm over very low heat until the chicken is ready to be served.

11. Check the doneness of the chicken by inserting a knife at the wing bone; if the juices run clear, it's finished cooking. Alternatively, you can use a meat thermometer to check that the temperature is at least 160°F. The vegetables should be softened but still toothsome.

12. Let the chicken rest for 10 minutes before serving.

13. While the chicken is resting, heat a skillet over medium heat and season the halved lemons with a touch of salt. Place the lemons cut side down in the hot skillet and char the lemon, undisturbed, until caramelized, about 3 minutes.

14. Serve the chicken with the roast vegetables and charred lemons. Pour some Parmesan broth over each serving.

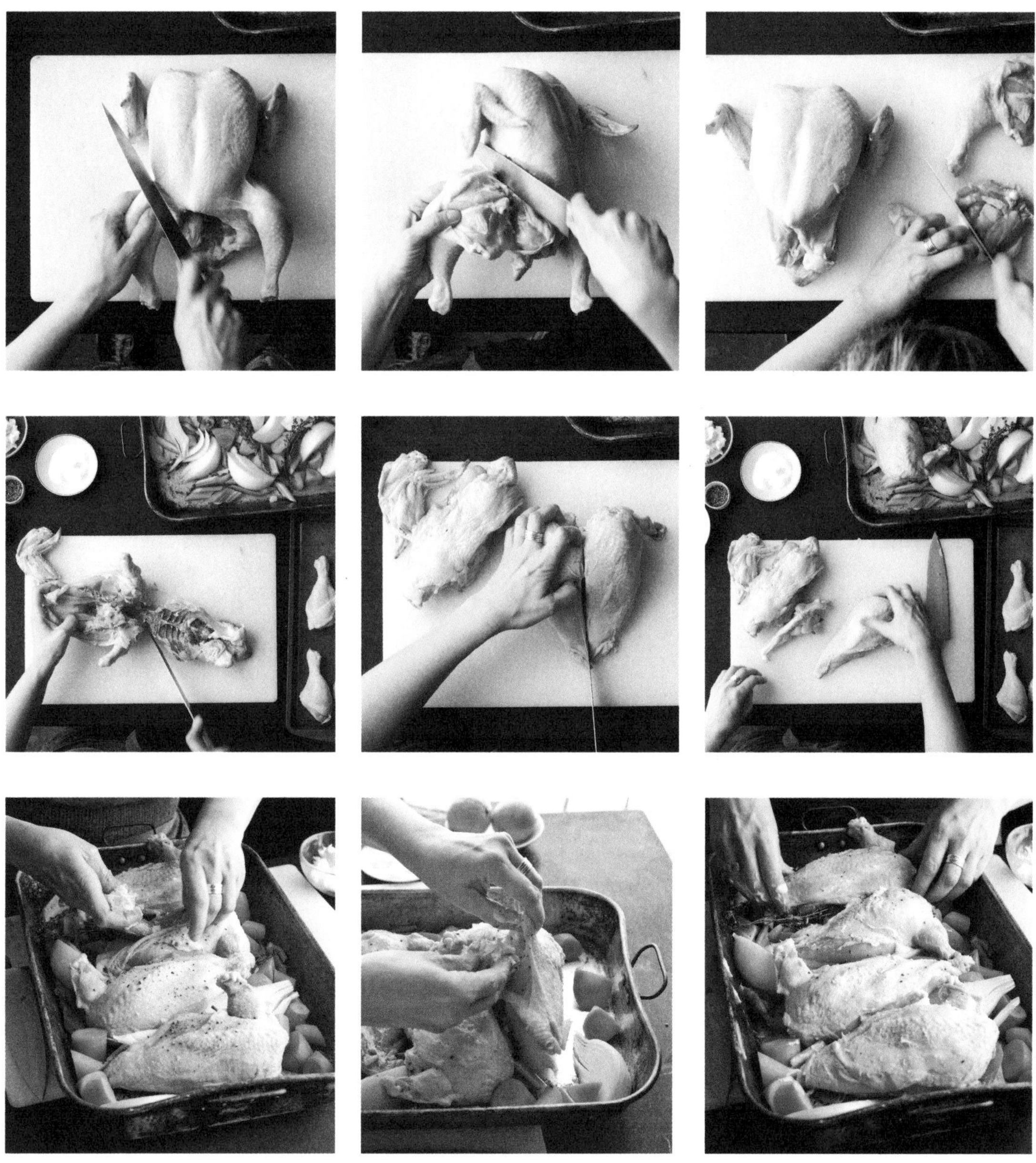

* Although breaking down a whole chicken might seem a bit messy, intimidating, or time-consuming, once you get the hang of it, you'll find it's the most cost-effective way to buy chicken—cut-up parts can double or triple the price. Plus you'll have the bones available to make homemade stock (see page 27), giving you even more bang for your buck!

LENTIL SOUP

MAKES 8 CUPS,
TO SERVE 4 TO 6

I started making myself this hearty lentil soup as a healthy answer to my comfort food cravings. I reached for lentils, kale, and sweet potatoes because they're a tasty trilogy of superfoods and chock-full of iron and energy. Luckily, they happen to play well together, resulting in a one-pot meal that always leaves me feeling satisfied—while I've done my body good!

- 6 tablespoons canola oil
- 1 yellow onion, diced
- 2 carrots, peeled and diced
- 2 celery ribs, diced
- 5 garlic cloves, sliced
- 2 teaspoons kosher salt
- 1 tablespoon tomato paste
- 2 cups dried lentils
- 10 cups Chicken Stock (page 27) or store-bought chicken or vegetable stock
- 1 sweet potato, peeled and cut into ½-inch dice
- 1 bunch green kale, coarsely chopped
- ¼ teaspoon cayenne pepper
- ½ teaspoon freshly cracked black pepper

PREP: PEEL AND DICE THE ONION, CARROTS, AND SWEET POTATO • DICE THE CELERY • PEEL AND SLICE THE GARLIC • CHOP THE KALE

1. Heat the canola oil in a large stockpot or Dutch oven over medium-low heat. Add the onion, carrots, celery, and garlic and season with 1 teaspoon of the kosher salt. Sweat the vegetables (cook over low heat, stirring frequently) until they begin to soften, about 8 minutes, taking care that they don't brown.

2. Add the tomato paste, stir, and cook for 2 to 3 minutes. Add the lentils and stock and turn up the heat to high to bring to a boil, then turn down the heat to maintain a low simmer and cook for 15 minutes. Add the sweet potato and continue to cook until the lentils are softened and tender, 20 to 25 minutes more.

3. Add the kale and stir, cooking until it has just begun to wilt into the soup, 3 to 4 minutes. Season with the cayenne, the remaining 1 teaspoon salt, and the black pepper. Stir again and serve hot!

* Normally you should avoid overcooking beans and legumes, but in this recipe undercooking is the worse sin. Even if you overcook the lentils a bit, the soup will be a success because the lentils will lend body and a creamy texture.

* The soup tends to thicken up in the refrigerator overnight, so when I have leftovers, I reincarnate it the next day as a side to a piece of fish or other lean protein. To reheat it for a bowl of soup, you might add a little more water or stock to the pot as it warms.

SALMON WITH PEAS, PEARL ONIONS, AND MINT

MAKES 4 SERVINGS

This is definitely a spring dish for me. After the endless bitter gray of our Northeastern winters, emerge from hibernation with delicate salmon, fresh spring peas, and mint. The flavors and colors of this dish scream spring, and the richness rounds it into a very satisfying meal. When fresh peas are not in season or unavailable, I reach for a bag of high-quality frozen peas, and fool even the most expert palates. My secret is out—I use frozen peas!

½ cup extra-virgin olive oil

1 cup peeled pearl onions (about 10 onions), halved

2 teaspoons kosher salt

1 teaspoon freshly cracked black pepper

2 cups fresh or frozen peas

1 cup chopped fresh mint leaves

4 (6-ounce) salmon fillets

Juice of 2 lemons

PREP: PEEL AND HALVE THE PEARL ONIONS • CHOP THE MINT • JUICE THE LEMONS

1. Preheat the oven to 350°F.

2. In a medium sauté pan over medium-high heat, heat ¼ cup of the olive oil and toss in the pearl onions. Season with 1 teaspoon of the salt and ½ teaspoon of the pepper and toss the onions to coat them in the oil. Sauté undisturbed until lightly browned, 3 to 4 minutes, then turn down the heat to low and cook until soft, 5 minutes more. Add the peas and mint and toss to combine. Remove from the heat.

3. In a large oven-safe sauté pan over high heat, heat the remaining ¼ cup olive oil. Season the salmon fillets with the remaining 1 teaspoon salt and ½ teaspoon pepper and add them to the pan, skin side down. Cook the salmon for 2 minutes, then move the pan to the oven and bake the salmon for 3 to 5 minutes, or until the skin is crispy and golden brown. It's okay if the salmon is still slightly pink in the middle.

4. Spoon the pea mixture into shallow bowls or dishes and top with the salmon fillets and a squeeze of lemon.

* **Home cooks are often more cautious than pro chefs and tend to cook fish and meat to a point that would be considered overcooked in a restaurant kitchen. This skin-side-down, stovetop-to-oven technique is often used on fish in restaurants to achieve a crispy skin with a moist interior.**

* **How do you keep proteins (fish, poultry, and meat) from sticking? You get a proper sear, whether in a pan or on the grill. The key to a proper sear is high heat. One of the biggest mistakes I see cooks make—even professional cooks—is being impatient when cooking meat or fish. If this means you need to turn your back and step away from the grill or oven to resist the urge to lower the heat or turn the protein before the hard sear is finished, then that's what you should do! The protein will tell you when it's time to flip, because it won't stick. Simple.**

BARLEY-STUFFED PEPPERS

MAKES 4 SERVINGS

This is an almost perfect dish for the home cook because it's economical, healthy, and scrumptious! You can whip it up anytime you have leftover cooked barley, brown rice, or quinoa from the night before. You could even reinvigorate a container of rice from last night's Chinese or Indian takeout! For a carnivore's take on this dish, add a cup of browned ground meat in place of 1 cup of the cooked barley or other grain.

¾ cup uncooked barley, or 2 cups cooked barley or other grain

2 tablespoons olive oil

2 cups sliced cremini mushrooms

Kosher salt and freshly cracked black pepper

½ cup grated Parmesan cheese

1 cup small-diced fresh mozzarella

¼ cup chopped fresh parsley

1 yellow bell pepper, halved lengthwise and seeded

1 red bell pepper, halved lengthwise and seeded

1 cup bread crumbs

PREP: SLICE THE MUSHROOMS • GRATE THE PARMESAN • DICE THE MOZZARELLA • CHOP THE PARSLEY • HALVE AND SEED THE BELL PEPPERS

The typical ratio for cooking barley is 1 part barley to 3 parts water or stock, but it's different for quick-cooking barley, so read the package.

1. Cook the barley according to the package instructions. Transfer the barley to a bowl and set aside.

2. Preheat the oven to 350°F and make sure the oven rack is positioned in the center.

3. In a large sauté pan, heat 1 tablespoon of the olive oil over medium-high heat. When the oil is hot and rippling, add half the mushrooms and season with a pinch of salt and a crack of black pepper. Do not touch the pan!

4. After 3 to 4 minutes, use tongs to flip one mushroom. If it's not browned to your liking, give them another minute or two. When they're ready, flip all the mushrooms and cook for another 2 to 3 minutes.

{ CONTINUED }

5. Add the cooked mushrooms to the bowl with the barley and repeat with the remaining mushrooms.

6. Add the Parmesan and mozzarella cheeses and the parsley to the bowl and stir to combine.

7. Line the pepper halves cut side up on a baking sheet and season each with a pinch of kosher salt.

8. Use a large spoon to divide the barley filling evenly among the pepper halves.

9. Place the baking sheet in the oven and bake until the filling is hot in the center and the peppers are tender, about 20 minutes.

10. Sprinkle the peppers with the bread crumbs and bake for 5 to 10 minutes more, or until the bread crumbs are golden brown.

---

* **It's important to let the mushrooms sear in this recipe. This is an old-school chef's secret—leaving mushrooms alone in an uncrowded pan over high heat ensures that they sear rather than steam, and you end up with the most delicious mushrooms ever as opposed to sad, bland, spongy, soggy, greasy mushrooms.**

* **Before adding any further seasoning to the mix, grab a spoon and taste! This is a very important step in cooking—tasting before seasoning—especially here, with two types of cheese involved, since cheese always lends saltiness to a dish. If you think it tastes great, then that's perfect—stop there. You're the chef and you're in control, so trust your own palate when it comes to seasoning.**

* **For added cheesy extravagance, you can also top each baked pepper with more cheese and place them back in the oven for 2 minutes, or until the cheese is golden brown and oozy.**

GRILLED STEAK WITH HERB BUTTER

MAKES 4 SERVINGS

I don't know if it's the same where you live, but a typical summer in New York City can get hot and steamy. When the mercury is rising and even the street seems to be sweating, it's hard to think about turning on the oven—which makes this grilled steak an ideal summertime meal. When partnered with seasonal tomatoes made sweet by the hot summer sun, a rich, flavorful herb butter, and the coldest beer I can find, this steak is one of my favorite meals for battling the dog days of summer. If tomatoes aren't in season, serve it with a warming side of creamed spinach (see page 202)—a classic pairing!

HERB BUTTER

1 cup (2 sticks) unsalted butter, at room temperature

1 shallot, minced

1 cup chopped fresh parsley leaves

1 teaspoon kosher salt

½ teaspoon freshly cracked black pepper

½ cup panko bread crumbs

STEAK

3 ripe beefsteak tomatoes

Kosher salt

Extra-virgin olive oil

4 (10- to 12-ounce) strip steaks

PREP: SET OUT THE BUTTER TO SOFTEN • MINCE THE SHALLOT • CHOP THE PARSLEY

{ CONTINUED }

1. To make the herb butter by hand: In a large bowl, combine the butter, shallot, and parsley, mixing well with a wooden spoon or rubber spatula until fully combined. Season with the salt and pepper, add the panko, mix again, and set aside.

   To make the herb butter in a food processor: Combine the butter, shallot, and parsley in the bowl of the food processor and pulse until blended. Scrape down the sides and bottom of the bowl to make sure the ingredients are thoroughly incorporated. Add the panko, salt, and pepper and pulse four or five times to mix. Transfer the herb butter to a bowl and set aside.

2. Heat an outdoor grill, a grill pan, or the broiler on high.

3. Cut the tomatoes into four slices each. Place three slices on each of four plates. Season with a pinch of salt and a drizzle of the extra-virgin olive oil.

4. Grill the steaks to your desired doneness (see tip), remove from the grill, and spread 1 or 2 tablespoons of the herb butter evenly on top of each steak.

5. Place one hot steak on top of each plate of seasoned tomatoes and serve.

* **Because of the variety of steak cuts and thicknesses, it's hard to dictate exactly how long it will take you to cook your steak. Don't be afraid to use a meat thermometer to get an accurate temperature reading on your steak. Otherwise, keep in mind that the more give the steak has when you poke it with your finger, the less cooked it is. For a steak that is about 1½ inches thick, you'll need about 12 minutes' cooking time—6 minutes for each side—to achieve medium-rare.**

* **Herb butters are just a version of compound butter (see page 44) and are a fantastically simple way to add fancy style and extra flavor to a variety of grilled dishes. They're not just for steak—experiment with different fresh herbs and match them with fish, chicken, or pork. Try dill butter with salmon, tarragon butter with chicken, or thyme butter with pork.**

* **If you can't find or don't have strip steaks, feel free to use another cut of steak—any will work. You can even use a larger cut, such as flank or skirt steak, and slice it to serve family-style on a platter over the tomatoes, or on individual plates.**

CORNMEAL-CRUSTED CHICKEN THIGHS WITH JAMAICAN SPICE

MAKES 4 SERVINGS

With the crunch of the cornmeal crust and kick of the Jamaican spice blend, this chicken is brimming with flavor and texture reminiscent of the much more time-consuming traditional Jamaican jerk marinade and fried chicken. If you're like me and love a lot of spice, feel free to add more cayenne pepper to the seasoning. Or if you prefer mild flavors, omit the cayenne completely. I like the dark meat of the chicken—it stays far juicier and tastier than the white meat—but feel free to use whichever you prefer.

½ cup instant polenta or finely ground cornmeal

2 teaspoons paprika

1 teaspoon ground allspice

1 teaspoon garlic powder

¼ teaspoon ground cinnamon

¼ teaspoon ground ginger

1 teaspoon ground coriander

½ teaspoon cayenne pepper

6 to 8 bone-in, skin-on chicken thighs

2 teaspoons kosher salt

1. Preheat the oven to 425°F.
2. In a wide, shallow bowl or dish, combine the polenta with the paprika, allspice, garlic powder, cinnamon, ginger, coriander, and cayenne. Use a fork or a whisk to mix well.
3. Season the chicken thighs with the salt, then coat them completely in the cornmeal-spice mixture.
4. Arrange the thighs skin side up in a shallow baking dish and bake for 15 minutes. Turn the oven temperature down to 350°F and cook for 15 minutes more, or until the juice of the chicken runs clear when you poke it with a fork.

* Stocking your pantry with a variety of spices really pays off in the flavor department. You'll always be ready to create unique spice blends that pack a flavor punch, and simple weeknight chicken can take you on a flavor trip to the Middle East, the Mediterranean, or, as in this recipe, the Caribbean.

* Try this chicken with mashed or baked sweet potatoes—or give it a summertime twist with Corn and Black Bean Salad (page 102).

* For a lower-fat version, use boneless, skinless thighs—just reduce the cooking time by 4 to 5 minutes at each heat level.

TOASTED QUINOA SOUP

MAKES 4 SERVINGS

This soup stems from my crazy quinoa obsession! Now that quinoa has become such a popular health food item, it's too easy to find it in bland, boring preparations, such as boiled and spooned on the side of a plate next to more interesting food. But when I was first learning about quinoa's health benefits, I stumbled across this soup, which is a version of a traditional Peruvian dish that's even sometimes eaten for breakfast! And here I was thinking I was the only one who ate quinoa for breakfast, because I always add it to my scrambled eggs.

Toasting quinoa adds a whole new flavor dimension to any quinoa dish and is a new technique to most.

1 cup uncooked quinoa
2 tablespoons olive oil
¼ cup diced onion
4 garlic cloves, sliced
¼ cup small-diced carrot
¼ cup small-diced red bell pepper
Kosher salt
1 teaspoon fresh rosemary leaves, minced
¼ teaspoon ground cumin
¼ cup small-diced peeled potato
6 cups vegetable stock or Chicken Stock (page 27)
½ cup small-diced zucchini

PREP: PEEL AND DICE THE ONION, CARROT, AND POTATO • DICE THE BELL PEPPER AND ZUCCHINI • PEEL AND SLICE THE GARLIC • MINCE THE ROSEMARY

1. Preheat the oven to 325°F. Spread the quinoa in a thin layer on a rimmed baking sheet and toast it in the oven until it completely changes color from beige to dark brown, about 30 minutes, using a spatula to stir it every 10 minutes to toast it evenly and keep the edges from burning. Set the quinoa aside.

2. In a large soup pot, heat the olive oil over medium heat. Add the onion, garlic, carrot, bell pepper, and a pinch of salt and sweat (cook over low heat, stirring frequently) for 10 to 12 minutes, until all the vegetables have softened. Add the rosemary and cumin and cook for 1 or 2 minutes, allowing the spices to bloom. Add the potato, toasted quinoa, and vegetable stock and stir.

3. Bring the soup to a boil, turn down the heat to maintain a simmer, cover, and cook for 30 minutes, or until the quinoa is tender. Add the zucchini and cook for 5 minutes more.

4. Taste the soup and adjust the seasoning as necessary.

* **Make sure you always rinse your quinoa in a fine-mesh strainer before cooking with it. Without rinsing it, you might find that the quinoa has a subtle bitter flavor.**

* **Make a big batch of this soup and freeze it and you'll always have a nutritious and tasty soup on hand when you need a dose of rejuvenation!**

KALE AND TOMATO STEW

MAKES 4 TO 6 SERVINGS

Here's a discovery I made when I started enjoying cooking for myself at home: I'm a closet vegetarian. I never really buy a big piece of meat and cook it just for me; usually I find myself making one-pot meals made up of delicious greens, beans, and grains. It's healthy, satisfying, and cheaper than buying meat every night—and I never feel as if I'm missing out. This stew is totally versatile and can be eaten with a fried egg on top or served under a piece of chicken or pork. But I mainly love it because it's so hearty and yummy as a solo act.

- 3 tablespoons olive oil
- 1 Spanish onion, peeled and cut into 8 wedges
- 1 teaspoon kosher salt, plus more as needed
- ¼ teaspoon chili flakes
- 6 garlic cloves, thinly sliced
- 1 large bunch green curly kale, ribs removed, leaves roughly chopped
- 3 cups drained canned or cooked chickpeas
- 4 cups chopped fresh plum tomatoes or canned stewed tomatoes, drained
- 1 cup vegetable stock
- ¼ teaspoon freshly cracked black pepper

PREP: PEEL AND CUT THE ONION • PEEL AND SLICE THE GARLIC • STEM AND CHOP THE KALE

1. In a large, wide saucepan or Dutch oven, heat the olive oil over medium heat. Add the onion, season with ½ teaspoon of the salt, and cook for about 3 minutes, or until slightly browned but not caramelized. Add the chili flakes and garlic and cook for 2 minutes. Add the kale and stir to coat it with the oil, onion, and garlic. Let it wilt down for about 1 minute.

2. Add the chickpeas, tomatoes, stock, and the remaining ½ teaspoon salt and cook for at least 10 minutes, allowing all the flavors to come together.

3. Season with more salt and the black pepper, and add more spice if you like an extra kick.

* Swiss chard is a great substitute for kale, and if you're feeling really leafy, try using BOTH!

* For an even deeper, cooked-all-day taste, use Roasted Garlic (page 15) instead of fresh garlic cloves.

PAN-SEARED TROUT WITH HORSERADISH CREAM

MAKES 2 SERVINGS

Prepared horseradish is oh so much more than just an addition to ketchup for cocktail sauce or tomato juice for a spicy Bloody Mary! Having horseradish on hand can jazz up a meal and rekindle your enthusiasm for weeknight fish, and this recipe proves it. Say good-bye to frozen fish fingers or boring sautéed fillets lacking sauce or flavor. This dish is just as quick but infinitely more satisfying. Be sure to ask your fishmonger to butterfly the trout to remove all the bones, making your weeknight cooking task a whole lot easier!

1 cup crème fraîche

½ cup prepared horseradish

¾ teaspoon kosher salt, plus more as needed

2 (10- to 12-ounce) whole trout

½ teaspoon freshly cracked black pepper

3 tablespoons canola oil

2 tablespoons fresh lemon juice

¼ cup fresh parsley leaves, chopped

PREP: JUICE THE LEMONS • CHOP THE PARSLEY

1. Combine the crème fraîche, horseradish, and ½ teaspoon of the salt in a small bowl and whisk together. Set aside.

2. Portion the trout by cutting them in half crosswise to create 4 steaks, not fillets. Both sides of the trout should still be attached in the center. Season with the remaining ¼ teaspoon salt and the pepper.

3. Place a large sauté pan over high heat and add the canola oil. When the oil ripples, carefully place the trout in the hot pan on one side of the skin, using tongs to lay the fish away from your body so the hot oil doesn't splash you. You should hear a beautiful sizzling sound as the fish hits the hot pan. If not, the oil isn't hot enough!

4. Cook for about 5 minutes on each side, making sure the skin gets beautifully crisp and golden brown.

5. In a small bowl, toss the lemon juice and parsley leaves together. Season with salt to taste.

6. To serve, you can simply spread the horseradish cream on a plate, top with two pieces of the trout, and sprinkle with the parsley salad. Or you can fancy it up by stacking the trout steaks and layering the horseradish cream and parsley salad in between.

* **If you have an awesome farmers' market or produce section that has fresh horseradish, lucky you! Just use the same amount of freshly grated peeled horseradish.**

* **Try sour cream or Greek yogurt in place of the crème fraîche.**

LOW AND SLOW

When I was in between restaurants and cooking a lot more at home, I was thrown off by all the extra time. Restaurant life is a real time and energy zapper, so I literally did not know what to do with myself at times. But once I got it together, I rejoiced in my newfound ability to enjoy some low and slow cooking. It didn't take long to get into the rhythms of putting something on the burner to get hot and bubbly while I took care of other chores, or even (dare I say it?) relaxed a little.

Now that I'm once again working as an executive chef, I'm making sure not to lose this habit. So when I do find myself at home with the rare luxury of time, I pour myself a glass of wine or grab an ice-cold beer and put together one of my favorite low-and-slow meals. They're among the most comforting dishes, harking back to the hearty, family-style meals with which a much-loved mother or grandmother filled our bellies and our hearts. Or, as is the case with Pop's Beer-Braised Bold Beef Stew (page 152), it conjures memories of my dad, methodically putting together and cooking his specialty as I looked on eagerly, hardly able to wait for the delicious result.

Cooking with time, low and slow, is a nice break from our usual harried day-to-day cooking. It's easy to fall into the trap of thinking that low and slow is time-consuming, but these meals can make the most sense when we're short on time, because their one common denominator—aside from tasting fantastic—is that you build them in one pot, pop it on the heat or in the oven or in a slow cooker, and forget about it for a few hours. Leaving you free to go about your business while dinner practically cooks itself.

Almost.

Low and Slow

JERSEY SUNDAY MEATBALLS

MAKES ABOUT THIRTY 3-OUNCE MEATBALLS, TO SERVE 6 TO 8

This is an ode to Jersey, and all the friends and neighbors with strong Italian roots who I grew up around. I have many warm childhood memories of a full belly after impressive Sunday suppers at their tables, filled with elegant yet humble and delicious dishes. After I became a chef, I traveled to Italy and observed similar practices and traditions all over the country, as families got together on Sundays for a big family meal, breaking bread and pausing to enjoy one another and some great food!

- 1½ cups panko bread crumbs
- 1 cup milk
- ½ pound ground veal
- ½ pound ground beef
- ½ pound ground pork
- 1 cup chopped shallots
- ½ cup minced garlic
- 1 teaspoon fresh thyme leaves, chopped
- ⅓ cup chopped fresh parsley leaves
- 1½ cups grated Parmesan cheese
- ¼ cup grated Pecorino Romano cheese
- 2 large eggs
- 1 tablespoon kosher salt
- Freshly cracked black pepper
- Olive oil, for searing the meatballs
- 1 recipe Marinara Sauce (page 35), for serving
- Pasta, for serving
- "Italian" Salad (page 100), for serving

PREP: MAKE THE MARINARA SAUCE • PEEL AND CHOP THE SHALLOTS • PEEL AND MINCE THE GARLIC • CHOP THE THYME AND PARSLEY • GRATE THE PARMESAN AND PECORINO ROMANO

Don't begin mixing the ingredients until they're all in the bowl. If you overmix, you'll end up with hockey pucks!

1. In a large bowl, combine the panko and milk. Let stand for 10 minutes, then add the veal, beef, pork, shallots, garlic, thyme, parsley, cheeses, eggs, salt, and pepper. Use your hands to mix and incorporate well.

{ CONTINUED }

2. Make a tester patty to taste for seasoning. This is a must! Simply sear a small amount of the meat, taste it, and adjust the seasoning in the rest of the mix as needed before you make the meatballs.

3. Take a small amount of the meat mixture in your hand—about ¼ cup or 3 ounces—and round it into a meatball that's about 3 inches wide. Place it on a baking sheet and continue to make the rest of the meatballs until you have used all of the meat mixture.

4. In a large sauté pan over high heat, heat enough olive oil to thoroughly coat the entire bottom of the pan (it should come about ¼ inch up the sides of the pan). In a separate saucepan, bring the marinara sauce to a simmer.

5. When the oil is hot and rippling, carefully fill the pan with as many meatballs as you can without overcrowding it. You have to work in batches so that the pan stays hot enough to really sear them. Turn the meatballs as you sear them, to ensure that they develop a nice brown caramelization on all sides, 3 to 4 minutes total.

6. As they're finished searing, place the meatballs directly into the simmering marinara.

7. Cook the meatballs in the marinara for about 45 minutes, then serve with pasta and "Italian" Salad.

*** Although I doubt you'll have leftovers, because these meatballs are so delicious, you can use any remaining meatballs and sauce for easy midweek meatball wedges (or hoagies or submarine sandwiches or whatever they're called where you live!).**

POP'S BEER-BRAISED BOLD BEEF STEW

MAKES 8 SERVINGS

Funny enough, of all the recipes in this book, this is the one closest to my heart and yet it was the hardest one to write anything about! My dad is no longer with us, but oh, how he loved making this stew. He had this very heavy cast-iron Dutch oven that he used every single time—and because nobody else in the house could lift it, this is the only recipe it was used for; my father was otherwise more of a pastry specialist! I have vivid memories of the hours he would spend meticulously pouring love into this stew—he even had his own way of cutting the onions, making sure to get perfect half-moon slices every time. He made it just a few times a year, and when it was on the menu, nobody in the family would miss dinner. Hours before the stew hit my mouth, I would already be salivating as the aroma of the slow-cooked onions, beer, wine, and beef filled every nook and cranny of the house. I have a sneaking suspicion that he tweaked it every time he made it, always trying to make it better—but we always thought it was perfect.

½ cup all-purpose flour

¾ teaspoon kosher salt

1 teaspoon freshly cracked black pepper

4 pounds chuck roast, cut into 1½-inch cubes (or have the butcher do it)

4 tablespoons (½ stick) unsalted butter

2 medium Spanish onions, diced

2 large carrots, peeled and diced

½ (750 ml) bottle red wine (about 1½ cups)—try a Cabernet Sauvignon or Zinfandel

2 bottles dark beer (Guinness or Negro Modelo)

4 cups low-sodium beef stock

1 pound peeled baby carrots (not pre-peeled, bagged "baby" carrots—real mini carrots!)

PREP: CUT UP THE CHUCK ROAST INTO CUBES (IF YOUR BUTCHER HASN'T DONE IT ALREADY) • PEEL AND DICE THE ONIONS AND CARROTS

{ CONTINUED }

1. In a medium bowl, combine the flour, ¼ teaspoon of the salt, and ½ teaspoon of the pepper and use a fork to mix well. Add the beef cubes and coat evenly with the seasoned flour. Transfer to a mesh strainer and shake off any excess flour.

2. Place a Dutch oven or a large heavy-bottomed pot over medium-high heat and add the butter. As soon as the butter melts and starts to foam, add the beef cubes in batches, in one even layer. Really let the beef brown on one side—3 to 4 minutes—then turn the meat with tongs and brown it well on the other sides.

3. Transfer the beef to a plate, leaving the butter and the flour solids in the pan. Continue browning the rest of the beef.

4. Add the onions and diced carrots to the pot and sauté over medium heat until they begin to caramelize, about 5 minutes.

5. Deglaze the pan with the wine (see tip), using a wooden spoon to scrape all of the browned bits from the bottom of the pot, and simmer until the wine has reduced by half, about 10 minutes. Add the beer and cook until reduced by half again, about 10 minutes.

6. Return the browned beef cubes to the liquid and cover with the stock. Bring to a simmer, then turn down the heat to low and season with the remaining ½ teaspoon salt and ½ teaspoon pepper. Cover and cook on low heat until the meat is fork-tender, about 2 hours, stirring occasionally to prevent it from scorching on the bottom.

7. Add the baby carrots and cover. Cook for another 30 minutes, or until they're tender. Taste and adjust the seasoning or add a bit more water if it has become too thick.

---

* **Have your butcher cube the chuck roast for you—having one less item on your prep list is never a bad thing.**

* **Feel free to use a quality store-bought beef stock, as long as it's a low-sodium version so you can control the salt in this stew. When the stock reduces, the flavors will concentrate—and that includes the sodium!**

* Those tasty bits of dried "gunk" that remain on the bottom of the pan or pot after browning meat are flavor gold. We know it as "fond" in the kitchen world; the term comes from the French word for sugar, because these bits are caramelized meat proteins, and they're the beginning of deliciousness. As long as they're not burned, they'll really help build flavor in your stew, so be sure to scrape them up with a spatula or wooden spoon when deglazing the pot with red wine.

* In busy restaurant kitchens, lids are either hard to find or nonexistent, so we use aluminum foil to fashion makeshift "lids" that really get the job done. If you do this at home, just be sure to wrap the foil around the rim of the pot to keep moisture from escaping as the stew cooks.

* Serve over Smashed Yukon Gold Potatoes (page 182).

CHICKEN FRICASSEE

MAKES 4 SERVINGS

Growing up, I watched my mom cook humble but soul-satisfying dishes like this fricassee in a slow cooker all of the time. I'm talking about the original Crock-Pot—it was ceramic and cream-colored with brown accent flowers, very hippie-chic. I'll admit that these days she's upgraded to a modern stainless-steel version, but the sight of this old-school Crock-Pot makes me smile—I had to have it! Lots of childhood food memories bubble away inside this old pot. And while the original brown, flowery slow cookers might have gone out of style, dinner at the push of a button certainly hasn't. Who doesn't need a few more hours in the day?

- 3 tablespoons olive oil
- 1 yellow bell pepper, julienned
- 1 red bell pepper, julienned
- 1 orange bell pepper, julienned
- 1 Spanish onion, diced
- 6 garlic cloves, diced
- 1 teaspoon ground cumin
- 1 teaspoon kosher salt
- ½ teaspoon freshly cracked black pepper
- 8 ounces beer (pilsner or lager works great) or white wine
- ½ cup tomato sauce or stewed tomatoes
- 1½ cups Chicken Stock (page 27)
- 20 green olives, pitted
- 5 small Yukon Gold potatoes, quartered
- 4 bone-in, skin-on chicken legs (about 3½ pounds)
- ¼ cup drained capers
- 2 limes, cut into wedges

PREP: SEED AND JULIENNE THE PEPPERS • PEEL AND DICE THE ONION AND GARLIC • PIT THE OLIVES • QUARTER THE POTATOES • CUT THE LIMES

SLOW COOKER

1. Combine all the ingredients except the capers and the limes in a slow cooker. Cook on high until it boils, then turn down to medium to simmer for 90 minutes, or until the chicken is tender and almost falling off the bone.

{ CONTINUED }

2. Add the capers and gently stir to incorporate.

3. Finish with a squeeze of lime just before serving.

STOVETOP

1. Heat the olive oil in a large Dutch oven or 8-quart stockpot over medium heat. Add the peppers, onion, and garlic and cook, stirring often, for 5 minutes, or until softened. You want no color on the vegetables.

2. Add the cumin, salt, black pepper, beer, tomato sauce, and stock. Stir and allow the mixture to simmer for a couple of minutes, then add the olives, potatoes, and capers.

3. Fit the chicken legs into the pot, skin side up, almost covering them with liquid, and bring to a boil. Turn down the heat to maintain a low simmer and cover the pot. Cook for 90 minutes to 2 hours, or until the chicken is practically falling off the bone.

4. Finish with a squeeze of lime over each portion to brighten the deep flavors.

* **I like to serve this dish with rice or pasta to soak up all the delicious broth that was created over the low-and-slow cooking time.**

PULLED PORK SANDWICHES

MAKES 4 TO 6 SERVINGS

On my culinary travels throughout the country, I've met and talked with a lot of proud chefs from big barbecue states about what makes their pulled pork great. The one thing I've learned is that there's no one best way. As with many aspects of barbecue, recipes and techniques for pulled pork are as varied and controversial as the sauce that should (or should not) go on top. In every reputable pork barbecue joint in this country, each plate seems to come with a story or tradition and an unwavering conviction that *this* is the best. However, you'll find one point of agreement anywhere you go: you can't make pulled pork in a hurry. But, oh boy, is it worth the wait.

3 tablespoons kosher salt

1 tablespoon freshly cracked black pepper

1 tablespoon chili powder

2 tablespoons light brown sugar

3 tablespoons vegetable oil

3 pounds boneless pork butt, cut into 4 equal pieces

2 onions, halved and sliced

1 jalapeño, thinly sliced (optional)

2 tablespoons apple cider vinegar

4 cups hard apple cider

4 to 6 brioche rolls

PREP: PEEL AND SLICE THE ONIONS • SLICE THE JALAPEÑO

1. Combine the salt, black pepper, chili powder, and brown sugar in a bowl and mix.

2. Use your clean hands to rub 2 tablespoons of the vegetable oil all over the pork, then do the same with the spice mix. Let the pork sit at room temperature to absorb the flavors for 20 minutes.

3. Heat the remaining 1 tablespoon vegetable oil in a heavy, high-sided, oven-safe pot or Dutch oven over high heat. Add the pork and brown it on all sides, 3 to 4 minutes per side.

4. Preheat the oven to 300°F.

{ CONTINUED }

5. Transfer the seared pork to a plate and turn down the heat to medium. Add the onions and jalapeño, if using, to the pan and sauté until the onions are translucent around the edges, 6 to 8 minutes.

6. Add the vinegar and apple cider to the pot and use a wooden spoon to scrape up all the caramelized bits at the bottom. Return the pork to the pot and cover. Carefully transfer the pot to the preheated oven.

7. Cook for about 3 hours, or until the pork is fully cooked and tender enough to be pulled apart with two forks. The pork will be hot, so carefully transfer it to a large cutting board or work surface, reserving the cooking liquid in the pot.

8. Use the two forks to pull all the pork apart. Transfer the shredded pork to a large bowl.

9. Use a large spoon or ladle to skim the fat from the very top of the braising liquid and discard the fat.

10. Add the braising liquid to the shredded pork and use tongs or a wooden spoon to coat the pork in the liquid.

11. Serve the pulled pork on the brioche buns.

* **Serve with Sweet and Spicy Chili Oil (page 38) to heat it up and No-Nonsense Coleslaw (page 193) to cool it back down.**

* **Slider buns make this a very easy game-day snack.**

PUERTO RICAN PERNIL

MAKES 4 TO 6 SERVINGS

I learned this dish from a pernil master—an expert Puerto Rican home cook in his Miami kitchen. I paid close attention, listened to his tips, and made mental notes so that I could re-create it. To learn traditional meals as special as this one, you must be there, looking on, learning the little tips and secrets that are singular to a cook's family tradition. I'm happy to share it with you and hope you treat it as the family heirloom it is, savoring every slice.

2½ tablespoons kosher salt

1 teaspoon freshly cracked black pepper

1 tablespoon dried oregano

¼ cup distilled white vinegar

5 or 6 garlic cloves

Juice of 5 limes

1 (4- to 5-pound) bone-in, skin-on pork shoulder or butt

PREP: PEEL THE GARLIC • JUICE THE LIMES

1. Place all the ingredients except the pork in a blender or the bowl of a food processor with ¼ cup water. Blend until smooth.
2. Use the tip of a paring knife or a large fork to carefully pierce holes all over the pork shoulder or butt. Rub the marinade all over the pork, letting it soak into the pierced areas. Transfer the pork to a large pan, cover, and refrigerate to marinate overnight.
3. Remove the pork from the fridge 2 hours before cooking so that it comes to room temperature.
4. Preheat the oven to 325°F.
5. Roast the pork in a large Dutch oven or high-sided roasting pan for 5 hours, uncovered, until the meat is very tender and almost falling off the bone.

Serve with a simple side of rice and beans, or make a "Cuban sandwich" with pork, pickles, mustard, and sliced ham on a warm bun.

TURKEY CHILI

MAKES 4 TO 6 SERVINGS

I can't remember ever enjoying a turkey burger—they're so not memorable. The lack of fat leaves them dry and unappetizing. Ground turkey is perfect in chili, though, because the spices and simmering braise infuse the turkey with flavor over time and make up for the lack of fat. You'll never miss it!

Cocoa powder adds a meaty richness that turkey meat cannot naturally offer. It adds a depth of flavor reminiscent of beef.

1 tablespoon canola oil

1 yellow onion, diced

Kosher salt

4 garlic cloves, thinly sliced

1 red bell pepper, diced

¼ cup chili powder

1 teaspoon ground cumin

¼ teaspoon cayenne pepper

2 tablespoons tomato paste

1 pound ground turkey

1 (28-ounce) can plum tomatoes

3 cups Chicken Stock (page 27) or low-sodium store-bought chicken stock, plus more as needed

1 tablespoon unsweetened cocoa powder

1½ cups cooked white beans, or 1 (12-ounce) can, drained and rinsed

1½ cups cooked kidney beans, or 1 (12-ounce) can, drained and rinsed

Optional garnishes: sour cream or plain Greek yogurt, sliced scallions, and grated Cheddar cheese

Try different kinds of beans in turkey chili for added flavor, texture, and color.

PREP: PEEL AND DICE THE ONION • PEEL AND SLICE THE GARLIC • SEED AND DICE THE BELL PEPPER • DRAIN AND RINSE THE CANNED BEANS

1. Heat the canola oil in a large pot or Dutch oven over medium heat. Add the onion and a pinch of kosher salt and sauté, stirring with a wooden spoon, for about 2 minutes, or until translucent. Add the garlic and bell pepper and sauté for 1 minute. Add the chili powder, cumin, and cayenne and cook for at least 1 minute so that they bloom.

2. Add the tomato paste and cook for 1 or 2 minutes to deepen its flavor.

3. Add the turkey and switch tools from a wooden spoon to a whisk. Cook the turkey, breaking up any large chunks with the whisk as you cook, for 5 minutes, or until browned.

A whisk is the perfect tool to break up raw ground meat.

4. Add the tomatoes, 3 cups of the stock, and the cocoa powder and bring to a simmer, whisking to make sure the cocoa powder is thoroughly dissolved and combined. Add the beans and bring the chili to a simmer.

5. Cover the pot with a lid or foil and cook the chili for 1 hour. Taste the chili after 1 hour and adjust the seasoning. If the chili is too thick for your liking, add a bit more chicken stock.

6. Serve in deep bowls topped with sour cream, sliced scallions, and grated Cheddar, if desired.

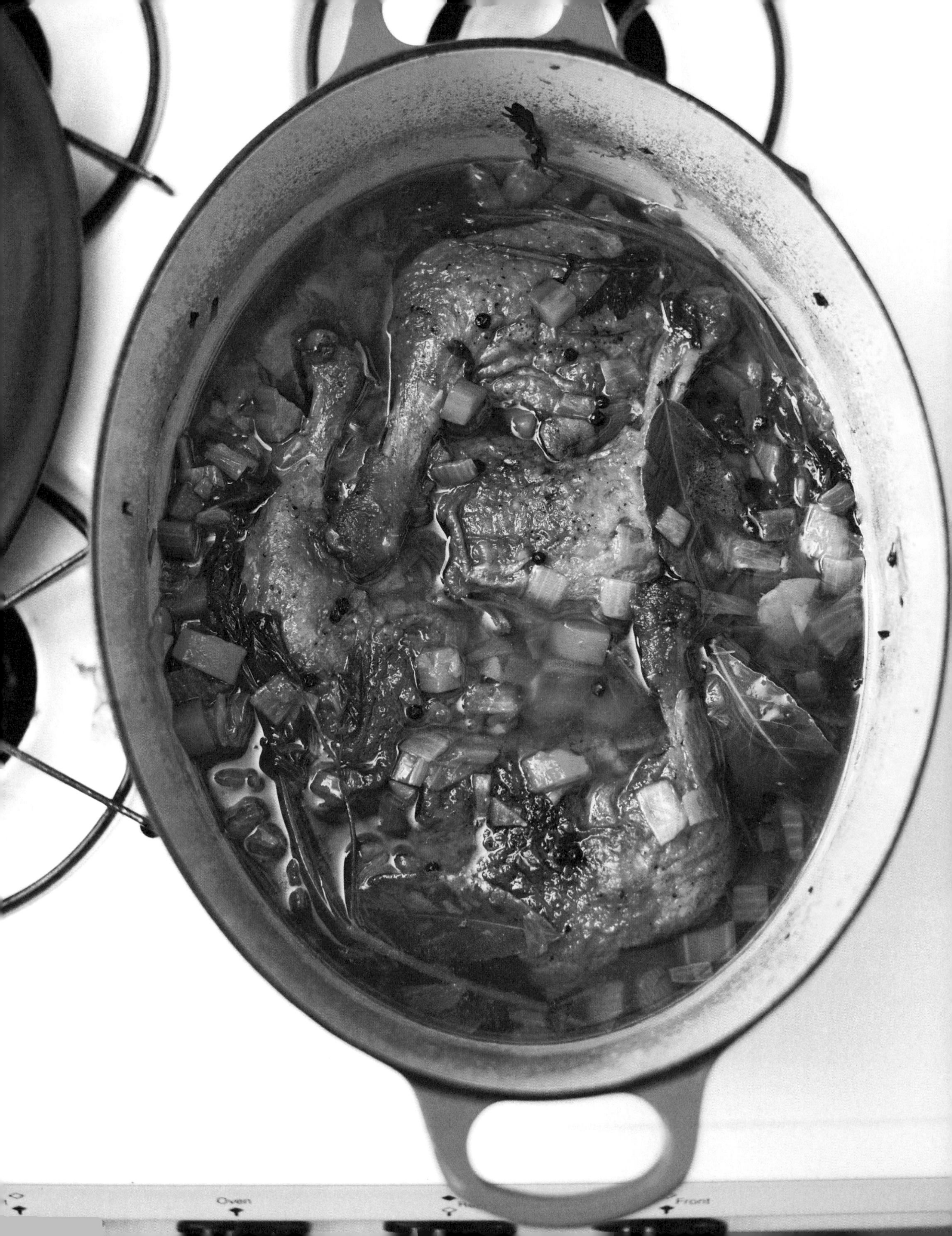
Oven
Front

WINTER DUCK LEG BRAISE

MAKES 4 SERVINGS

Many people might think of a beautifully seared duck breast as the most elegant incarnation of duck, perhaps because it's what you find most often on restaurant menus. While there's no doubt that a perfectly seared duck breast is a wonderful thing, there's something to be said about the warmth and scrumptiousness of braised duck legs. If you're thinking of making duck for the first time, this is a great starter recipe. The braising process is more forgiving than a straightforward seared duck breast but will still give you the opportunity to practice rendering the fat, which is arguably the most important step when working with duck, no matter the preparation.

4 uncooked duck legs (about 7 to 8 ounces each)

1 teaspoon kosher salt

½ teaspoon freshly cracked black pepper

½ cup olive oil

1 large carrot, peeled and cut into 1-inch dice

2 celery ribs, cut into 1-inch pieces

1 large onion, cut into 1-inch pieces

12 large garlic cloves, halved

1 cup red wine (Chianti is preferable, but you can also use Cabernet Sauvignon)

4 cups Chicken Stock (page 27)

20 whole black peppercorns

2 bay leaves

8 fresh parsley sprigs

PREP: PEEL AND CUT THE CARROT AND ONION • CUT THE CELERY • PEEL AND HALVE THE GARLIC

Don't throw out the fat—refrigerate it in a covered container and use it for roasting potatoes or veggies later in the week.

1. Generously season the duck legs with the salt and cracked pepper.

2. Heat the olive oil in a heavy-bottomed braising pot or Dutch oven over medium-high heat. When the oil is very hot, carefully lay the duck legs skin side down in the oil, slowly rendering the fat from the skin. After the initial sear, turn down the heat and use a small ladle or deep spoon to remove the excess fat as it collects in the pot.

{ CONTINUED }

3. When the skin is dark golden brown, 10 to 12 minutes, turn the legs and cook for 1 minute.

4. Transfer the duck legs to a paper towel–lined plate or baking sheet to drain any excess fat. Remove all but 2 tablespoons of the fat remaining in the pot.

5. Add the vegetables and garlic to the pan and sauté until the vegetables are just beginning to brown, 3 to 4 minutes.

6. Preheat the oven to 350°F.

7. Add the wine and simmer on high for about 20 minutes, or until the liquid has reduced to a quarter of its volume.

8. Add the stock, peppercorns, bay leaves, and parsley. Bring to a boil, then turn down the heat to maintain a simmer and cover. Place the pot in the oven and cook for about 1½ hours (see tip).

9. Check the duck legs—if they are fork-tender, they're ready. Remove the legs and let them rest on a plate.

10. Strain the sauce through a fine-mesh strainer or colander and discard the solids. Return the strained liquid back to the pot and cook over medium heat until it has reduced to your preferred sauce consistency.

11. Taste the sauce and season as desired. Serve the sauce with the duck legs.

* **The time it takes to cook the duck legs will depend very much on the size of the legs; use this as a guideline, but if the duck legs you have are on the smaller side, they may cook in just an hour.**

* **Straining and reducing the sauce will make this dish closer to what you might find in a restaurant.**

* **It's important not to add salt or pepper before reducing a sauce, as the flavor concentrates and you could end up with a too-salty sauce. Always taste and adjust the seasoning after reducing.**

POTATO-KALE SOUP

MAKES 8 CUPS,
TO SERVE ABOUT 6

The idea behind this soup is to build a deeply flavorful base, and while using both Spanish onions and leeks may seem like onion overkill, the kale gives it a beautiful, fresh finish. I love all manner of potato soups, even the über-fancy chilled vichyssoise. This version is a bit of a cross between that and the more rustic Portuguese-style potato-kale soup that has chunks of smoked Portuguese sausage in it. I wanted to keep this recipe vegetarian, but you can certainly garnish with chorizo or any sausage you like to turn this into a meaty meal. Regardless, serve it with crusty bread and I promise it won't leave you hungry. Each satisfying bite will warm you from the inside out.

Be sure to wash leeks extremely well! The layers can be loaded with sand and soil.

2 tablespoons canola oil

2 Spanish onions, diced

10 garlic cloves, coarsely chopped

1 leek, cleaned and thinly sliced

2 teaspoons kosher salt, plus more as needed

1 pound Yukon Gold potatoes, peeled and diced

6 cups vegetable stock or Chicken Stock (page 27)

¾ pound Tuscan or curly kale, ribs removed, leaves coarsely chopped

½ teaspoon freshly cracked black pepper

Optional garnishes: hot paprika, extra-virgin olive oil

PREP: PEEL AND DICE THE ONIONS • PEEL AND CHOP THE GARLIC • CLEAN AND SLICE THE LEEK • PEEL AND DICE THE POTATOES AND PUT THEM IN A BOWL OF COLD WATER • STEM AND CHOP THE KALE

Use a lid to contain all the steam and get a nice "sweat."

1. Heat the canola oil in a large, wide saucepan over medium-low heat. Add the onions, garlic, and leek, season with 1 teaspoon of the salt, and sweat (cook over low heat, stirring frequently) until the vegetables are cooked down and really soft with no color, up to 10 minutes.

2. Add the potatoes, stock, and remaining 1 teaspoon salt and simmer over low heat until the potatoes are fully cooked, about 30 minutes.

{ CONTINUED }

3. Let the potato-leek mixture cool to room temperature, then puree it in a food processor or blender, working in batches as needed, or directly in the pot with an immersion blender, until completely smooth.

4. Return the puree to the original saucepan and bring it to a simmer over medium heat. Stir in the kale and season with salt and pepper.

5. Serve the soup in deep bowls and garnish with a sprinkle of hot paprika and a drizzle of olive oil, if desired. Enjoy with a wedge of crusty bread.

*** If you don't like leeks, sub in sliced yellow onions or even a few large sliced shallots.**

BEEF SHORT RIBS

MAKES 4 TO 6 SERVINGS

For a long time, you'd find short ribs in restaurants but not often on home cooks' menus. But it's become more fashionable to use cheaper cuts of meat, so they're now widely available in almost every supermarket and definitely at every butcher. The chef's secret here is that short ribs can deliver bold flavor and elegance for much less money than a good steak; the only compromise is that you need the low-and-slow technique to make them shine. Cooking short ribs is not as simple as putting a prime cut of steak on the grill, because you need to coax the flavors out gently. This dish is sure to impress your family and guests and give you the platform to show off your "cheffy" skills, even though you and I will know that the most important ingredient was time.

5 pounds bone-in beef short ribs, 2 inches thick

Kosher salt and freshly cracked black pepper

1 tablespoon canola oil

1 large carrot, peeled and cut into 8 pieces

2 onions, peeled and cut into 8 pieces

1 turnip, peeled and cut into 8 pieces

3 garlic cloves

2 tablespoons tomato paste

1 cup red wine

6 cups beef stock

PREP: PEEL AND CUT THE CARROT, ONIONS, AND TURNIP • PEEL THE GARLIC

1. Preheat the oven to 350°F.
2. Generously season the ribs with salt and pepper.
3. In a large heavy-bottomed pot or Dutch oven, heat the canola oil over medium-high heat. Once the oil is hot and rippling, carefully add the short ribs to the pot and sear until well browned on all sides, about 2 minutes per side. Work in batches as needed so as not to crowd the pot; you need the heat high enough to really sear the ribs.
4. Remove the ribs from the pot with tongs and set them aside on a baking sheet.

{ CONTINUED }

5. Carefully pour off all but about 3 tablespoons of the fat remaining in the pot.

6. Turn down the heat to medium and add the cut vegetables and the garlic to the pot. Season with salt and pepper. Sauté until the vegetables begin to brown slightly, 3 to 4 minutes. Add the tomato paste and cook until it begins to turn a deeper shade of red, 3 to 4 minutes.

7. Deglaze the pot with the wine and use a wooden spoon to scrape up the caramelized bits from the bottom of the pot. Simmer until the wine has reduced by half.

8. Add the beef stock, bring it to a boil, and return the ribs to the pot. Add water as needed to cover.

9. Cover the pot and put it in the oven. Braise the ribs for 3½ hours, or until fork-tender, soft, and nonresistant.

---

* **Serve atop Root Vegetable Puree (page 200) or alongside Smashed Yukon Gold Potatoes (page 182).**

* **For an added splash of color and crunch, try them with Green Beans with Toasted Almonds (page 185) or blanched asparagus (see page 9).**

CORNED BEEF AND CABBAGE

MAKES 6 SERVINGS

My mom's Irish roots might be pretty far down on the tree, but on St. Patrick's Day she breaks them out as an excuse to have her corned beef and cabbage. She cooked it every St. Paddy's Day when I was growing up, and still keeps the tradition alive—a treat I look forward to every year. This is a version of the corned beef and cabbage that my mom and I have cultivated over the years, through lots of trial and error. Some years we used the wrong size pot, or the wrong cooking time, or the wrong kind of beer, or the wrong combination of spices, but this recipe is the compilation of all of the things we did right every year—our perfect corned beef and cabbage.

3 pounds corned beef brisket

3 cups beer

2 tablespoons whole coriander seeds

4 whole cloves

4 bay leaves

¼ cup whole black peppercorns

1 teaspoon ground allspice

¼ cup whole mustard seeds

4 carrots, peeled and quartered

1 pound fingerling potatoes

1 small green cabbage, trimmed and cut into 6 wedges

In my experience, dark beers such as Guinness don't work well here—stick to pilsners and lagers for cooking Corned Beef.

PREP: SCRUB THE POTATOES • PEEL AND QUARTER THE CARROTS • TRIM AND CUT THE CABBAGE

1. Place all the ingredients except the potatoes and cabbage into a large stockpot. Add enough water to cover the corned beef.

2. Bring to a boil over high heat, then turn down the heat to maintain a simmer and tightly cover with a lid or aluminum foil. Cook for 5 hours, or until the corned beef is fork-tender.

3. About 30 minutes before the corned beef is done, add the potatoes and cabbage. They should be cooked through and tender.

4. Serve with crusty whole-grain bread and lots of grainy mustard.

* Substitute any baby potatoes for the fingerlings. If you use larger potatoes, cut them into large chunks—roughly four pieces per potato. Whether you peel them or not is up to you!

* This may seem like a lot of corned beef, but a leftover corned beef sandwich is second to none. Pile it high on pumpernickel or rye bread and slather it with All-Around Mustard Sauce (page 47).

SIDES

Sautéed veggies. Boiled rice. Baked potatoes. Each has its place and all are perfectly acceptable side dishes—but they're also a tiny bit boring. Sometimes, I find the easiest way to shake it up at mealtime isn't by changing the star of the show but rather by switching up the supporting cast. A side of zesty Mediterranean potato salad or sinfully rich creamed spinach will elevate a simple grilled chicken breast or baked fish in a way that boiled potatoes or sautéed spinach do not.

In my battle to feel comfortable in my home kitchen, one of my biggest obstacles was a lack of inspiration. When I was time crunched and hungry, the sound of my grumbling belly drowned out my creativity. The bag of potatoes I had just bought went straight into the boiling salted water, and the head of broccoli was destined only for the sauté pan. But once I got my footing, I began to have fun with my side dishes. I realized that they hold the power to bump up a meal to restaurant level without you having to make yourself too crazy. This chapter is full of side dishes that I hope will inspire you to think outside the box when it comes to rounding out your meals—and I think you'll find that they keep cooking interesting, not just for the eaters but for the cook, too!

Sides

ROASTED CAULIFLOWER

MAKES 4 SERVINGS

Cauliflower is easily underestimated. When it is simply steamed or blanched, the result is white and watery, without any flavor pizzazz or color. But when roasted, cauliflower is transformed from vegetable wallflower to attractive life of the party! This recipe is both straightforward and simple, but the key is how you cut the cauliflower. It's important to cut it in cross sections rather than florets. This way you can exploit the flat surface area of each piece, which will allow for maximum caramelization and a burst of flavor in every nook and cranny! And the turmeric in the recipe gives you golden cauliflower with lovely browned edges.

1 head cauliflower

2 tablespoons olive oil

1 teaspoon ground turmeric

1 teaspoon kosher salt

¼ teaspoon freshly cracked black pepper

PREP: TRIM THE LEAVES AND THE END OF THE CORE FROM THE CAULIFLOWER

1. Preheat the oven to 450°F.
2. Cut the cauliflower in half, from top to bottom. Cut each half from top to bottom in half-inch cross sections, resulting in a mixed bag of whole cauliflower "steaks" and flat florets. This is one of the very few cases where it's okay to cut a vegetable into different sizes, because the width will be more or less the same whether you have a whole "steak" or smaller pieces.
3. Transfer the cauliflower to a baking sheet large enough to comfortably accommodate all the pieces with a little space to spare, or use two baking sheets, or cook in two batches.
4. In a small bowl or measuring cup, combine the olive oil, turmeric, salt, and pepper. Use a fork or whisk to combine well. Drizzle the spiced olive oil over the cauliflower. Use your best tools (your clean hands) to coat the florets, covering them completely.

{ CONTINUED }

5. Place the baking sheet(s) in the center of the oven and roast for 20 to 30 minutes, rotating the baking sheet halfway through to ensure even browning. The cauliflower should be a beautiful yellow color from the turmeric and nicely browned on the edges from the caramelization.

*** Don't overlook the nibbly bits that remain on the cutting board after you prep the cauliflower! Throw them on the baking sheet, too, and they'll become browned, crunchy bits of flavor goodness—almost like mini cauliflower croutons!**

SMASHED YUKON GOLD POTATOES

MAKES 4 SERVINGS

Yukon Golds are appropriately named because of their buttery taste and golden color. They really need very little dressing up, but the scallions and sour cream in this recipe elevate them from your standard spud. In this recipe, they are as rustic as can be—somewhere between boiled and mashed. This dish is the solution for the time-crunched cook's mashed potato.

- 2 pounds Yukon Gold potatoes, unpeeled
- 2 tablespoons kosher salt, plus ¼ teaspoon for seasoning
- ½ cup Chicken Stock (page 27) or vegetable stock
- 1 cup finely chopped scallions
- Freshly cracked black pepper
- 1 cup sour cream

PREP: SCRUB THE POTATOES • CHOP THE SCALLIONS

1. Place the potatoes in a large stockpot and add enough water to cover and the 2 tablespoons salt. Bring the water to a boil over high heat and cook the potatoes until fork-tender, about 25 minutes. Drain the potatoes.
2. Return the potatoes to the still-warm pot and add the stock. Using the back of a wooden or metal spoon, roughly smash the potatoes to expose the flesh. Add the scallions and season the potatoes with the remaining ¼ teaspoon salt and pepper to taste. Add the sour cream and stir to incorporate it completely.
3. Transfer the potatoes to a serving dish and crack some additional pepper over the top before serving.

* This recipe would also work well with Red Bliss, Idaho, or even sweet potatoes! Try Greek yogurt instead of sour cream to lighten it up, and/or use chives instead of scallions.

* Serve with Pop's Beer-Braised Bold Beef Stew (page 152), Grilled Steak with Herb Butter (page 135), or "Lusty" Lemon Chicken (page 125).

GREEN BEANS WITH TOASTED ALMONDS

MAKES 3 CUPS,
TO SERVE ABOUT 4

It may not be a new idea, but green beans with almonds is a classic that never goes out of style in my house. This is my easy and flavorful spin on the traditional dish that goes with just about anything, but beware—since the first ingredient is one whole stick of butter, it's certainly not for anyone on a diet!

½ cup (1 stick) unsalted butter
2 shallots, thinly sliced
1 cup raw sliced almonds
1 pound string beans, trimmed
¼ teaspoon kosher salt
Freshly cracked black pepper

PREP: TRIM THE STRING BEANS • PEEL AND SLICE THE SHALLOTS

You're making brown butter, which goes from nutty and golden to burned very quickly—so pay attention!

1. Blanch the string beans in boiling water using the technique on page 9.
2. In a 14-inch sauté pan, heat the butter over medium-high heat, letting it get foamy and light brown.
3. Add the shallots and almonds and toast them in the butter for 1 to 2 minutes, or until warmed through and coated with the butter.
4. Add the beans and use tongs to toss them around in the pan. Season with the salt and a crack of pepper.
5. This dish is great when served family-style on a large platter. Serve a heaping pile of green beans, topped with the almonds, shallots, and brown butter.

CORNBREAD AND CHALLAH STUFFING

MAKES 6 SERVINGS

I guess in some parts of the country this recipe might be called dressing rather than stuffing because it's not cooked inside a turkey. In my house, stuffing was the universal term for the yummy mixture of stock-soaked bread, vegetables, butter, and herbs baked and served nicely crisped on top but still perfectly moist in the center. I did a lot of research on the stuffing-versus-dressing debate while writing this recipe because I wasn't sure what to call it! Apparently this question resonates with a lot of people, and their opinions are based in personal family food traditions, which I love.

So call it what you like—stuffing or dressing. Whatever the name, it tastes delicious whether it's on your Thanksgiving table or the highlight of a chilly autumn night. It's sure to satisfy the soul.

Nonstick cooking spray

1 loaf challah bread, cut into cubes (about 4 cups)

4 cups cubed corn bread

½ cup (1 stick) unsalted butter

2 onions, diced

4 celery ribs, diced

6 garlic cloves, sliced

⅓ cup chopped fresh sage leaves

½ cup chopped fresh parsley leaves

4 cups Chicken Stock (page 27), plus more as needed

2 teaspoons kosher salt

1 teaspoon freshly cracked black pepper

PREP: CUBE THE BREADS • PEEL AND DICE THE ONIONS • DICE THE CELERY • PEEL AND SLICE THE GARLIC • CHOP THE SAGE AND PARSLEY

1. Preheat the oven to 350°F. Spray a 9 × 13-inch roasting pan with nonstick cooking spray.
2. Place the challah and corn bread cubes on separate rimmed baking sheets and toast them until lightly browned and dry, about 10 minutes. Transfer the bread cubes to a large bowl.

3. Melt the butter in a large sauté pan over medium heat. Add the onions, celery, and garlic and cook until translucent, 10 to 12 minutes.

4. Add the sage, parsley, and chicken stock and bring to a boil. Season with salt and pepper and stir. Cook for 1 minute, then pour the stock mixture over the bread in the bowl. Use a large spoon to mix the stuffing thoroughly.

5. Transfer the stuffing to the prepared roasting pan, pressing down on it lightly to nestle it into the pan and distribute it evenly.

6. Bake for 45 minutes to 1 hour, until nicely browned on top but still moist inside. Serve warm.

---

* **If you can't find challah, go for buttery, soft breads like hamburger rolls, hot dog buns, or brioche.**

OLIVE OIL MASHED POTATOES

MAKES 3 CUPS,
TO SERVE ABOUT 4

I created this recipe for my two nieces, who eat dairy-free but still like to explore a wide range of dishes and flavors. They're little culinarians who love to eat and be in the kitchen with Aunt Amanda. I don't know who enjoys it more—me or them! I have a distinct memory of the first time I let my niece Megan pour the olive oil into the potatoes as they mixed in the stand mixer. My brother and sister-in-law looked on, afraid she'd lose a hand to that thing! (She didn't.)

4 Idaho potatoes, peeled and cut into large equal-size chunks

¼ cup plus ¾ teaspoon kosher salt

¼ cup extra-virgin olive oil

¼ teaspoon freshly cracked black pepper

PREP: PEEL AND CUT THE POTATOES

1. Place the potatoes in a medium saucepan and add cold water to cover. Add ¼ cup of the salt to season the water well. Cook over medium-low heat until fork-tender, about 20 minutes, depending on the chunk size. Drain the potatoes and set aside to cool slightly.
2. Transfer the potatoes to the bowl of a stand mixer fitted with the whisk attachment. Add the olive oil and mix on low speed until soft.
3. Season with the remaining ¾ teaspoon salt and the pepper.

* **If you don't have a stand mixer, use a potato masher or ricer to soften the cooked potatoes in a large bowl and then add the olive oil, using a combination of the potato masher and a rubber spatula to mix well.**

GIARDINIERA

MAKES 2 QUARTS

As a sucker for pickled anything, I never turn down giardiniera, in any form. Whether it is the often overlooked component of a big Italian antipasti platter or just straight out of a jar, I can't get enough of this stuff. I am usually the only one passing over the array of cured meats and cheeses to grab a big pickled cauliflower floret. So this recipe comes from a quest to make my own perfect version to have on hand at all times.

- 1½ to 2 cups distilled white vinegar
- 1½ to 2 cups white balsamic vinegar
- 2 to 3 tablespoons sugar
- 1 to 2 bay leaves
- 1 tablespoon fennel seeds
- 2 tablespoons kosher salt
- 1 head cauliflower, trimmed and cut into florets
- 2 large carrots, peeled and cut into 1-inch rounds
- 3 or 4 celery ribs, diced
- 1 red bell pepper, seeded and cut into 1-inch dice
- 2 Fresno chiles, seeded and cut into 1-inch dice
- 3 or 4 garlic cloves

PREP: TRIM AND CUT THE CAULIFLOWER • PEEL AND CUT THE CARROTS • DICE THE CELERY • SEED AND DICE THE PEPPER AND CHILES • PEEL THE GARLIC

1. In a large saucepan, combine the vinegars, sugar, bay leaves, fennel seeds, and salt. Stir well to combine and bring to a boil over medium heat.
2. When the sugar has dissolved completely, turn off the heat and add all the vegetables.
3. When the liquid has cooled, transfer the vegetables and liquid to a suitably sized mason jar or any combination of tightly sealed containers, making sure the liquid covers the vegetables.
4. Place in the fridge to chill for at least 2 hours before eating.

* Since there's no sanitizing or boiling of jars involved here, these pickles have to live in the fridge—they're not shelf stable. But they will last in the fridge for at least a couple of weeks, as long as the vegetables remain covered with the pickling liquid and the container is tightly sealed.

* If your food tastes are at all like mine, you'll devour these pickled vegetables straight out of the jar on a whim. But they lend a refreshing crunch as a side dish at a summer BBQ, or chopped up on top of Italian sandwiches. Or put them out alongside Mixed Marinated Olives (page 70) for an impressive yet simple snack with cocktails or drinks.

NO-NONSENSE COLESLAW

MAKES 6 TO 8 SERVINGS

Because I hail from New Jersey, a state known for its amazing diners, it's no surprise that I ate my first coleslaw alongside a burger in one of those little white pleated paper cups. If you're familiar with those cups, you know they hold only about two ounces of coleslaw, so I never really got my fill! This is my version of a straightforward New Jersey diner coleslaw. No nonsense, just how we like it in Jersey.

1 head green cabbage, shredded (about 4 cups)

1 cup shredded carrots

1 shallot, thinly sliced

½ cup thinly sliced celery

¼ cup distilled white vinegar

2 tablespoons sherry vinegar

½ cup canola oil

1½ tablespoons sugar

1 garlic clove, thinly sliced

½ cup mayonnaise

2 teaspoons kosher salt

½ teaspoon freshly cracked black pepper

PREP: SHRED THE CABBAGE • PEEL AND GRATE OR SHRED THE CARROTS • PEEL AND SLICE THE SHALLOT AND GARLIC • SLICE THE CELERY

1. In a large bowl, combine the cabbage, carrots, shallot, and celery. Set aside.
2. Combine the vinegars, oil, sugar, garlic, and mayonnaise in a medium bowl. Add the salt and pepper and whisk to combine.
3. Add the dressing to the slaw and use a wooden spoon or rubber spatula to toss and combine well, coating the shredded vegetables thoroughly with the dressing.
4. Allow the slaw to develop flavor and wilt for at least 1 hour at room temperature ahead of serving.

BROCCOLINI WITH LEMON AND ROSEMARY

MAKES 4 SERVINGS

I love anything in the broccoli family, particularly broccolini. It's a delicious hybrid vegetable that offers the vibrant crunch of broccoli but also the tenderness you want in a raw salad. This sauce is based on an Italian sauce called *salmoriglio* that includes garlic, lemon, and olive oil. Enough said. Serve as a jazzed-up side vegetable or over pasta. If you find yourself with leftovers, chop them up and use them as a sandwich condiment the next day!

- 1 bunch broccolini, trimmed
- 4 garlic cloves, sliced
- ¼ teaspoon chopped fresh rosemary
- ½ teaspoon chili flakes
- 1 teaspoon grated lemon zest
- ¼ cup fresh lemon juice (from 2 lemons)
- ¼ cup olive oil
- ⅛ teaspoon kosher salt

PREP: TRIM THE BROCCOLINI • PEEL AND SLICE THE GARLIC • CHOP THE ROSEMARY • ZEST AND JUICE THE LEMON

1. Blanch the broccolini using the technique on page 9.
2. Combine the rest of the ingredients in a bowl and whisk together.
3. Pour the sauce into a large sauté pan and gently warm it over low heat, slightly cooking the garlic and blooming the chili flakes.
4. Add the broccolini and coat it with the warm sauce, making sure all the florets are dressed.

* **Broccoli rabe and standard broccoli both work well in this preparation.**

ORZO PASTA SALAD

MAKES 3 CUPS, TO SERVE 4

This basic pasta salad may seem passé, but I still love it! There are so many great Mediterranean flavors in here, united by pasta—what could be better? Orzo cooks very quickly, so be sure to keep a watchful eye on it while it is on the stove. Also, cooking the orzo is a big-time seasoning opportunity. If you fail to salt the pasta water appropriately, the orzo itself will be bland and you'll have to compensate for it at the end, which will result in a salty dish rather than a perfectly seasoned one. So don't season the water with a pinch of salt—season it so it tastes like the ocean!

¾ cup uncooked orzo

Kosher salt

¼ cup diced red onion

¼ cup chopped pitted black olives

¼ cup chopped fresh parsley

¼ cup crumbled feta cheese

¼ cup red wine vinegar

¼ teaspoon chopped fresh oregano

1 tablespoon chopped fresh basil

2 tablespoons grated Parmesan cheese

¼ cup extra-virgin olive oil

½ cup cherry tomatoes, halved

Freshly cracked black pepper

PREP: PEEL AND DICE THE ONION • CHOP THE OLIVES, PARSLEY, OREGANO, AND BASIL • GRATE THE PARMESAN • HALVE THE CHERRY TOMATOES

1. Prepare the orzo according to the package directions, taking care to salt the water generously. Drain and set aside to cool to room temperature.
2. In a large bowl, combine the orzo with the rest of the ingredients and ⅛ teaspoon salt. Use your clean hands or two large spoons to mix it carefully. Taste and adjust the seasoning if necessary.
3. Refrigerate the pasta salad for at least 15 to 20 minutes before serving.

* **Serve alongside burgers and grilled meats at an outdoor BBQ or top with a protein for a quick lunch or dinner.**

MEDITERRANEAN POTATO SALAD

MAKES **4** SERVINGS

This potato salad is similar to a classic German potato salad in that the basis for the dressing is olive oil and vinegar rather than mayo. But the flavors here are distinctly Mediterranean—briny with a hint of citrus and spice.

- 1½ pounds fingerling potatoes
- ¼ teaspoon kosher salt, plus more for cooking the potatoes
- 1 cup extra-virgin olive oil
- 4 Fresno chiles, seeded and finely diced
- 2 teaspoons cayenne pepper
- 1 cup sliced garlic cloves
- ¼ cup capers in brine, undrained
- ¼ cup (2 lemons) fresh lemon juice
- ¼ cup white balsamic vinegar

PREP: SCRUB THE POTATOES • SEED AND FINELY DICE THE CHILES • PEEL AND SLICE THE GARLIC

1. Cook the fingerling potatoes in boiling salted water until just tender enough to easily pierce with a knife or fork, 12 to 15 minutes. Drain and let cool just enough that you can safely handle them. Peel and slice the potatoes into equal 1-inch rounds (see tip). Transfer the potatoes to a medium bowl and set aside.

2. In a small sauté pan over medium-low heat, gently heat the olive oil along with the chiles, cayenne, garlic, and salt, cooking until the garlic just begins to turn a light golden brown, about 3 minutes.

3. Remove the pan from the heat and add the capers in their brine, lemon juice, and white balsamic vinegar. Pour this mixture over the potatoes and marinate at room temperature for about 2 hours.

4. Taste and adjust the seasoning as needed just before serving. Garnish with parsley.

* Try this dish as a complement to Herb-Stuffed Whole Fish (page 241).

* Don't make yourself crazy trying to peel tiny potatoes like fingerlings before cooking. When you slice them after they're cooked, the peel will usually come off naturally. Any skin that remains can be either left on or scraped off with the back of a paring knife.

* I like to use Fresno chiles a lot in my cooking because I like spice, but I also like the flavor of sweet peppers. Fresnos offer the heat of a jalapeño and the sweetness of a red bell pepper, so it's the best of both worlds and gives a well-rounded pepper flavor to any dish. But you could also use jalapeños or red bell peppers as substitutes in this dish.

ROOT VEGETABLE PUREE

MAKES 2 CUPS,
TO SERVE ABOUT 4

The key to root vegetable purees is achieving a perfect velvety texture; there's nothing worse than a lumpy puree. Just as you'd add milk and butter to mashed potatoes, cream and butter play a big role in getting that silky smoothness here. So just embrace it, and remember all of the vitamins and nutrients you're getting from the veggies to balance it out!

2½ cups medium-diced butternut squash

½ cup small-diced celery root

1 cup medium-diced turnip

¼ cup kosher salt, plus more for seasoning

2 tablespoons unsalted butter

⅓ cup heavy cream

This may seem like a lot of salt, but don't freak out. Your root vegetables will end up perfectly seasoned, and most of the salt will go down the drain.

PREP: PEEL AND DICE THE VEGETABLES

1. Place all the vegetables in a large saucepan and add water to cover. Season the water with ¼ cup salt. Cover and bring to a boil over medium-high heat. Turn down the heat to maintain a simmer and cook until tender, 15 to 20 minutes.

2. Drain the vegetables in a colander and set aside to cool briefly.

3. In a small saucepan, combine the butter and heavy cream over low heat. Remove from the heat when the butter has melted and the mixture is warm (do not simmer).

4. Transfer the vegetables and butter-cream mixture to the bowl of a food processor or blender and blend until smooth. You might have to do this in batches.

5. Taste the puree and adjust the seasoning if necessary. Serve warm.

* Serve with Beef Short Ribs (page 171), Pop's Beer-Braised Bold Beef Stew (page 152), or Duck Breast with Pine Nut Relish (page 247).

* Sub sweet potatoes for the butternut squash or parsnip for the celery root.

CLASSIC CREAMED SPINACH

MAKES 8 CUPS, TO SERVE 8 TO 10

I can't resist a pat-on-my-back moment here—I rock at making creamed spinach. And I'm sharing this recipe with you because I want you to feel the same kind of confidence. Hidden in this seemingly straightforward recipe are lots of skills and foundational techniques, such as making a roux and a béchamel and sautéing onions. When you master this, you can say you're awesome at cooking—and you're definitely ready to graduate to the next chapter ("The Scary Stuff"!). Plus, this steakhouse classic is a great way to get everyone chowing down on iron-rich spinach.

2 pounds baby spinach

½ cup (1 stick) unsalted butter

½ cup diced Spanish onion

2 tablespoons minced garlic

2¼ teaspoons kosher salt

½ cup all-purpose flour

2½ cups milk

1 cup heavy cream

⅛ teaspoon freshly grated nutmeg

⅛ teaspoon cayenne pepper

Use whole nutmeg freshly grated with a Microplane when possible. Like many whole spices, nutmeg dies a pretty quick death when ground before it's needed.

PREP: THOROUGHLY WASH THE SPINACH • PEEL AND DICE THE ONION • PEEL AND MINCE THE GARLIC

1. Blanch the spinach using the technique on page 9. Drain in a colander and set aside to cool.

2. Use your hands to press the spinach against the sides of the colander. When most of the liquid has been released, squeeze handfuls of the spinach to make sure all of the excess water has been removed. Set aside.

3. In a wide, high-sided sauté pan, melt the butter over medium-low heat. Add the onion, garlic, and a pinch of kosher salt and sweat the vegetables (cook over low heat, stirring frequently) until they are soft, about 6 minutes.

4. With a wooden spoon, stir the flour into the butter, onion, and garlic mixture to create a roux that will look like wet sand. Cook the roux for 3 minutes, stirring continuously to make sure it doesn't burn.

It's important to cook your roux, or you'll end up with a raw-flour taste in your spinach.

5. Add the milk to the roux, whisking vigorously to make sure that the roux completely dissolves into the milk without lumping.

6. Turn down the heat to maintain a low simmer. You're making a béchamel sauce, which is the base for the creamed spinach. Cook the béchamel for 3 minutes, then whisk in the cream and return the mixture to a simmer.

7. Add the spinach to the béchamel, folding to make sure it's completely coated with sauce. Season with the nutmeg and cayenne.

8. Cook for 2 minutes, then taste the spinach. Adjust the seasoning with more salt, nutmeg, and/or cayenne if desired.

---

* **This béchamel sauce is a classic French mother sauce, the basis for many sauces and dishes, including mac and cheese and fondue. The darker the roux, the more nutty and intense the flavor it will give a sauce. Here the roux doesn't need to be cooked further than a light, or blond, color.**

* **Serve with Grilled Steak with Herb Butter (page 135), "Lusty" Lemon Chicken (page 125), or just about any grilled or roasted meat.**

THE SCARY STUFF

Some dishes and techniques are simply more intimidating than others. With a little organization and prep, anyone can find success in the kitchen, but there are some dishes that might not be worth the undertaking at home, however good a cook you are. Finding success in the kitchen is often about understanding your boundaries and limitations as much as it's about quality ingredients and correct seasoning. But our first instinct is usually to blame ourselves when a dish goes horribly awry. *My palate is unrefined. I followed the recipe exactly and it still didn't come out the way it looks in the picture. I'm obviously just not a good cook. I could burn water.* Sound like the voice in your head? But often, cooking success has nothing to do with your ability to follow a recipe—it's about recognizing your limitations and embracing them.

Timing. Equipment. Space. These are three of the main potential pitfalls in a kitchen, even for professional chefs, and they're at least as critical for home cooks to consider. Whether you're boiling store-bought pasta or making multistep *arancine* (rice balls), if you don't get the timing right, the dish will be unsuccessful. Similarly, if you don't own a mandoline and your potato gratin dish requires a slew of finely sliced potatoes at the same exact thickness, you're doomed before you start. Puff pastry is notorious for monopolizing time and space (not to mention sanity). You have to be meticulous to get it right, and it also requires lots of room to spread out—room that I don't have. So I never make it at home, and that's okay!

Rather than position yourself for failure by attempting a dish that will be tricky given your home kitchen setup, choose something else. I do this all the time. When I'm in the restaurant's kitchen, I have multiple ovens, both regular and convection. But at home my one oven is standard and tiny—so I'll never cook a meal with components that need oven heating at the same time. The scary stuff becomes a whole lot less scary when you understand your resources. This will help with planning as well as cooking.

Here I've included recipes that I think can be intimidating for home cooks. There may be a difficult cooking technique, or a foreign or exotic element, one you think you can't pronounce, let alone cook. But many seemingly complicated techniques aren't actually that hard, such as cooking and breaking down a lobster or searing scallops perfectly. So I've written these recipes to really help you go for it, paying special attention to details of time, space, and equipment—not to mention technique—to make sure they're definitely doable for the home cook.

On days when you have a bit more time to play in the kitchen, or aren't under pressure to cook for guests, or are just feeling a bit more adventurous—these are definitely the recipes to try!

The Scary Stuff

MARINATED ARTICHOKES

MAKES 3 QUARTS

When was the last time you bought a raw, whole artichoke? I'm guessing that for most of you, the answer is never. And I don't blame you—with their pointy, off-putting leaves and fuzzy, weird-looking inner chokes, they're just about the most intimidating vegetable in the grocery store. I mean, what part do you even eat? The heart? The leaves? It's hard to know where to start, so in the interest of instilling some confidence, I thought we should take baby steps and start with baby artichokes. Their small size makes them inherently more tender and edible, requiring a smidgeon less preparation than their full-grown relatives. And once you feel comfortable with the smaller artichokes, you can tackle the big guys, because the basic preparation is the same—and the results are delicious.

- 6 lemons, halved crosswise
- 16 baby artichokes
- 3 tablespoons plus ½ teaspoon kosher salt
- 4 cups plus 2 tablespoons olive oil
- 2 garlic heads, halved crosswise
- 1 bunch fresh thyme
- 1 bunch fresh tarragon
- 1 cup white wine

PREP: HALVE THE LEMONS • HALVE THE GARLIC HEADS

TRIMMING THE ARTICHOKES

1. Fill a large pot with cold water and squeeze 3 of the lemons into it (this is known as acidulated water). Keep it off the heat for now. The cut artichoke hearts have to head straight for the lemon water to keep them from browning.

2. Lay an artichoke on its side and trim the brown, woody tip of the stem. Using a very sharp or serrated knife, cut the top one-third of the thorny artichoke leaves off, leaving a flattened top.

3. Use your hands to tear off the toughest outermost leaves from around the bottom of the artichoke, leaving most of the leaves untouched.

4. Lay the artichoke on the board again and this time cut it in half lengthwise, from top to tip.

{ CONTINUED }

5. Using a paring knife or a peeler, carefully peel off the outermost layer of the stem.

6. Use a spoon to scrape away the inedible furry "choke" in the center of the artichoke.

7. Voilà—you have an artichoke heart! Quick, put it in the acidulated water!

8. Repeat to trim the rest of the artichokes.

POACHING THE ARTICHOKES

1. Add more water to the pot if needed to cover the artichokes. Season the water with 3 tablespoons of the salt.

2. Place the pot over medium-low heat and bring the water to a simmer. Poach the artichokes for about 15 minutes, or until they're easily pierced with the tip of a knife.

3. Drain the artichokes. Transfer them to a large bowl and set aside.

MARINATING THE ARTICHOKES

1. In a medium saucepan, heat 2 tablespoons of the olive oil over medium-low heat. Add the garlic halves, cut side down, and sear them until lightly golden, 3 to 4 minutes.

2. Add the thyme and tarragon. Squeeze the remaining 3 lemons into the pan and throw in the squeezed lemon halves as well.

3. Add the wine and simmer on high heat until it has reduced by half, about 5 minutes.

4. Add the remaining 4 cups olive oil and the remaining ½ teaspoon salt. Bring the marinade to a boil, then turn off the heat. Carefully pour the hot marinade over the artichokes and stir to combine.

5. Transfer the artichokes and marinade to mason jars with lids or airtight containers and refrigerate. Marinate the artichokes for at least 1 hour, but ideally overnight, before serving. Store them in the refrigerator for 1 week to 10 days.

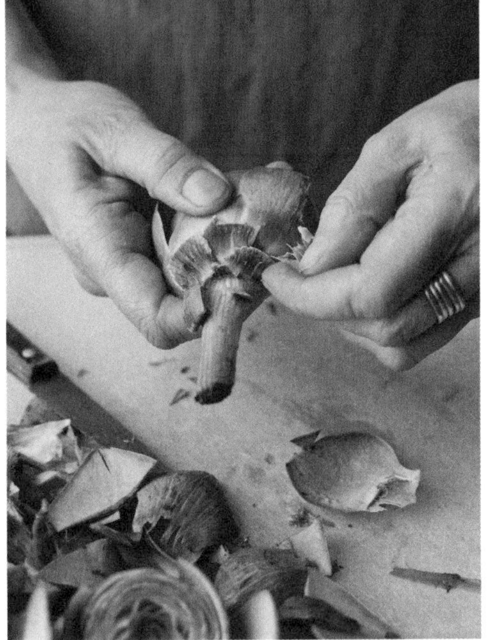

* When you're buying artichokes, grab the ones with the most tightly packed leaves.

* If you can't find baby artichokes, use the large ones instead. To make an equivalent batch for this recipe, you'll probably need 6 large artichokes.

OVEN-ROASTED LOBSTERS

MAKES 4 SERVINGS

This dish was inspired by a photo in *The River Café Cook Book* by Rose Gray and Ruth Rogers of the famous restaurant in London. I've always admired the simplicity of their cooking, and glancing through the book I saw the photo of a roasted lobster, split open with herbs on top. I can honestly say I never even read the recipe—at the time I was working in a restaurant with a wood-burning oven and I just saw a great opportunity, so I came up with my own version.

The tough part is always the lobsters. I don't mind working with live lobsters, but somehow they do always manage to cut or poke my hands with the spiny parts on their heads . . . it must be revenge. So I always use kitchen towels when handling them.

I'm well aware that a lot of people aren't comfortable with killing lobsters; it can be a little scary the first time. But get in there and try it—I promise that in the battle of cook versus lobster, the cook always wins!

Four 1½-pound lobsters—alive!

1½ cups (3 sticks) butter or Easy Compound Lemon-Pepper Butter (page 44), at room temperature

PREP: ASSEMBLE TOOLS: CHEF'S KNIFE, KITCHEN TOWELS, LOBSTER CRACKER

1. Place a lobster facedown on a board. You'll have to hold it down with a kitchen towel, because it usually fights back.

2. Use a large, sharp-pointed knife to split the lobster completely in half by inserting the knife at the head and cutting in half directly down the center to the tail.

3. Use your fingers to remove the stomach sac found in the head and crack the claws with a lobster cracker in a few places. Don't expose the meat; just crack the claws so that you can easily remove the meat when the lobster is cooked. Repeat with a second lobster.

4. Preheat the broiler to 500°F.

5. Place the lobster halves cut side up on a rimmed baking sheet and slather the meat with half the butter.

{ CONTINUED }

6. Repeat this process with the other 2 lobsters on a second baking sheet.

7. Roast the lobsters for about 15 minutes, one sheet at a time. The shell will turn red and the butter will melt, bathing and flavoring the meat. Serve immediately.

* **Serve this lobster on a bed of creamy Basic Risotto (page 3).**

* **The lobsters can also be cooked on a grill in the summer, or if you are lucky enough to have a wood-burning oven—use that!**

HEARTY GNOCCHI

MAKES 4 SERVINGS
(10 GNOCCHI PER SERVING)

Well-made gnocchi are a thing of beauty. If the gnocchi are light and pillowy, not heavy and dense, you know you've nailed it. As with homemade pasta, making gnocchi is not necessarily difficult, just a bit intimidating. You might have to practice a couple of times before you get the feel for making this dough, but once you do, you'll be cooking batches of homemade gnocchi for everyone! The beauty of gnocchi—as with stuffed pastas—is that once you've made the gnocchi, the "hard" work is done. They don't require fussy or complicated sauces—in fact, the opposite is true. Dress them in a simple brown butter sauce flavored with a few whole fresh sage leaves and you have the definition of fast and delicious.

2 large Idaho potatoes

1 teaspoon kosher salt, plus more for cooking the potatoes and gnocchi

½ cup all-purpose flour, plus more for dusting

2 large egg yolks

½ teaspoon freshly cracked black pepper

Brown butter sauce: Wide sauté pan over medium-high heat—1 stick butter, melt until foamy and brown, add fresh sage, sauté 1 or 2 minutes, remove from heat, add gnocchi.

1. Place the unpeeled potatoes in a medium saucepan and add water to cover. Salt the water, then bring it to a boil and cook the potatoes until fork-tender, about 35 minutes.

2. Drain the potatoes and let them cool to a point where you can safely handle them. It's best to make the gnocchi dough while the potatoes are still slightly warm. While the potatoes are cooling, lightly flour a baking sheet and cover it with a slightly damp towel.

3. Using a paring knife, carefully peel the potatoes. Pass them through a potato ricer or push them through a colander into a large bowl.

4. Add the flour, egg yolks, salt, and pepper and use your clean hands to combine the mixture, being careful not to overmix.

{ CONTINUED }

Work as fast as possible with the warm dough so that it doesn't dry out before you cut the gnocchi.

5. Turn the dough out onto a clean, lightly floured surface. Separate roughly 1½ cups of dough, a little larger than a tennis ball.

6. Use your hands to roll the dough back and forth until it forms a 1-inch-thick log.

7. With the tip of a chef's knife, cut the log into 1-inch pieces. Place the gnocchi on the prepared baking sheet as you finish them. Repeat with the rest of the dough. One batch of dough should yield roughly 6 to 8 logs.

8. Bring a large pot of salted water to a boil over high heat. Drop the gnocchi into the water. When they float, after about 2 minutes, they are done.

9. Drain and serve immediately with your sauce of choice.

*** Try the gnocchi with Marinara Sauce (page 35), Fresh Tomato Sauce (page 43), or Sweet Summer Corn Sauce (page 56).**

*** While potato ricers are ubiquitous in professional restaurant kitchens, they're less common in home kitchens. If you're like me and find yourself without a potato ricer at home, then push the potatoes through the bottom of a colander. This method is ideal because it lets the potatoes retain their natural fluffiness, and this air contributes to a light gnocchi. Potatoes mashed the old-fashioned way will result in dense gnocchi.**

*** Save your egg whites in a clean, airtight container for up to 1 week and add them to your next omelet or frittata—try Spinach, Potato, and Ricotta Egg White Frittata (page 119).**

*** This recipe is best eaten when fresh!**

BUTTERMILK BISCUITS

MAKES TWELVE 3-INCH BISCUITS

I have so much respect for all the cooks in this country who have perfected their biscuit-making skills. To this day, I still sometimes have difficulty making light, airy, flaky biscuits. Yes, it's relatively simple to put the dough together—the trick is handling the biscuits delicately. Puff pastry is a classic French pastry that intimidates some of the most experienced chefs, and many of the same foundational techniques apply to making biscuits, so it's no surprise that biscuits can be difficult to master. In my experience, any recipe that includes flour, butter, and a leavening agent such as baking soda can be touchy because a good result depends on minimal handling, time for the dough to rest, and the correct ingredient temperatures. For example, the butter must be cold, but since your hands are warm and you use your hands to mix the dough, it's a tricky situation. But it's entirely possible to become an expert biscuit baker—it just requires practice and a little bit of patience.

3 cups all-purpose flour

1 tablespoon baking powder

½ teaspoon baking soda

Rounded ½ teaspoon kosher salt, plus more for sprinkling

1 teaspoon freshly cracked black pepper

1½ cups (3 sticks) unsalted butter, cold, cut into small cubes

1 cup well-shaken buttermilk, cold

Nonstick cooking spray

1 tablespoon heavy cream, cold

Sugar (optional), for sprinkling

1. Combine the flour, baking powder, baking soda, salt, and pepper in a large bowl. Cut in the butter with a pastry cutter or rub it in using your clean hands until the mixture is in chickpea-size crumbs.

2. Add the buttermilk and use a wooden spoon to bring the dough together. It's very important not to overmix the dough here!

3. Lay out a piece of plastic wrap large enough to enclose the dough and transfer the dough from the bowl onto the plastic. Wrap the dough in the plastic and place in the fridge to chill for 1 hour.

4. Unwrap the dough and transfer it to a lightly floured surface. Use a rolling pin to roll out the dough 1 inch thick.

5. Grease a baking sheet with nonstick cooking spray.
6. Punch out the biscuits with a biscuit cutter and transfer them to the prepared baking sheet, spacing them about 1 inch apart.
7. Refrigerate the biscuits on the baking sheet for 15 minutes.
8. Preheat the oven to 400°F.
9. Brush the tops of the biscuits with the cream and sprinkle each with a pinch of sugar, if desired, or salt.
10. Bake for 12 to 15 minutes, or until golden brown.

SEARED SCALLOPS

MAKES 12 SCALLOPS
(6 APPETIZER SERVINGS OR
4 ENTRÉE SERVINGS)

The first thing to know before making this recipe—which is barely even a recipe, more of a technique for a simple and elegant dish—is to take down your smoke alarm. Okay, maybe don't do that, because it's unsafe. But definitely open the windows and turn on a fan, because you need to have a screaming-hot pan to achieve beautifully sweet sea scallops with a perfectly caramelized sear. A pro kitchen is equipped with 30,000 BTUs of gas and indestructible stainless-steel pans, and we're not afraid to use them. Gird your loins, turn up the heat, and you'll have a chance of capturing scallop magic at home.

12 sea scallops, cleaned

Kosher salt and freshly cracked black pepper

2 tablespoons canola or vegetable oil

1 lemon, cut into wedges

PREP: REMOVE THE ADDUCTOR MUSCLE FROM EACH SCALLOP • CUT THE LEMON

Make sure the adductor muscles are removed before you cook the scallops because they're inedible and unpleasant to chew. Ask your fishmonger if you need help the first time.

1. Place a layer of paper towels on top of a large plate or baking sheet and gently lay the sea scallops on top to rid them of any excess moisture. With the scallops still on the paper towel, grab a large pinch of kosher salt and sprinkle it from a foot or more over the scallops. The height will help distribute the salt evenly.

2. Use a pepper grinder to crack fresh black pepper in the same manner, getting every scallop.

3. Flip the scallops and season the other side. This is important!

4. Heat the oil in a large cast-iron skillet or heavy-bottomed stainless-steel sauté pan over high heat. Do not use nonstick—you'll never achieve the proper caramelization!

   Wait.

   Wait.

   Watch as the pan begins to smoke.

{ CONTINUED }

If the scallops are crowded in the pan, it will cool too quickly to sear them properly. If you think your pan isn't wide enough to comfortably accommodate all the scallops, work in batches—or risk soggy scallops.

5. Now, carefully, because the pan and oil are very hot, use tongs or your fingers to place each scallop individually in the pan, leaving room between them. Once the scallops are in the pan, do not move them or the pan or turn the heat down. You're going to want to, because the pan will be hot and splattering and smoking, but resist! You're getting your hard sear. Don't interfere or the scallops will stick.

6. After 2 minutes, use a spatula or tongs to gently turn one of the scallops and assess how dark the sear is. If it's dark brown and caramelized, it's ready to be flipped and seared on the other side for at least 2 minutes more to achieve an identical sear.

7. When the scallops have been flipped and seared on both sides, they're fully cooked and ready to eat. Remove them from the pan using tongs or a spatula and serve them hot with a simple squeeze of fresh lemon juice on top.

* **Shopping for the best ingredients is almost as important as the cooking technique you use, and never is this more true than with sea scallops. Often at the fish market you'll see sea scallops marked either "dry" or "wet." Ask for the dry scallops if they're available; you'll never be able to attain the same hard sear on the wet scallops.**

CORN SOUFFLÉ

MAKES FOUR 8-OUNCE RAMEKINS,
AS SIDE SERVINGS

This dish is inspired by a soufflé restaurant in San Francisco named Cafe Jacqueline. Just imagine! All soufflés, all the time! I had a very memorable three-course soufflé meal there with my friend Pam before getting on a plane back to New York. If I had to indulge in a three-course meal just before a flight, one that consists only of soufflés was the right call. They were light as air—leaving us satisfied but not overly stuffed. The perfect feeling to have before boarding a plane.

- 4 tablespoons (½ stick) butter, plus more for the ramekins
- 1 cup corn kernels (fresh or frozen)
- 1 teaspoon minced garlic
- ⅛ teaspoon cayenne pepper
- 3 tablespoons all-purpose flour
- 1½ cups milk
- 4 egg whites
- ½ teaspoon kosher salt

PREP: CUT THE CORN KERNELS FROM THE COB (IF USING FRESH) • PEEL AND MINCE THE GARLIC • SEPARATE THE EGGS, RESERVING THE WHITES

1. Melt 4 tablespoons of the butter in a medium saucepan over medium-high heat. Add the corn kernels, garlic, and cayenne and sauté for 2 to 3 minutes, or until the corn starts to brown.

2. Sprinkle in the flour and use a wooden spoon to stir continuously, making sure the flour doesn't stick to the bottom of the pan. Cook for 2 to 3 minutes to remove any raw flour taste.

3. Turn the heat down to medium-low and slowly pour the milk into the pan, continuing to vigorously stir, preventing lumps. Cook, stirring, for about 5 minutes, or until thickened, and add the salt. This is the béchamel base for the soufflé.

4. Transfer the béchamel to a bowl to cool. It's important that it cool completely.

{ CONTINUED }

5. Preheat the oven to 450°F. Generously butter the bottom and sides of four 8-ounce ramekins.

6. In the bowl of a stand mixer fitted with the whisk attachment, or with a hand mixer, whip the egg whites until they form stiff peaks.

7. Incorporate half the egg whites into the cooled soufflé, gently folding them in with a rubber spatula or wooden spoon. Fold in the rest of the egg whites, turning the bowl as you bring the mix from the bottom up and over, up and over, until thoroughly mixed.

8. Gently divide the soufflé batter among the ramekins. Bake for 18 minutes, then check for doneness. Using the oven light is ideal, because if you open the oven door to check their progress, they may collapse. When the soufflés have doubled in size and risen over the rim of the ramekins, they're ready to serve!

*** Serve the soufflés immediately—but if one falls after it emerges from the oven, don't let your confidence deflate along with it! This particular soufflé recipe is meant as a baby step toward your soufflé mastery—it's not super-touchy and won't rise to superfancy heights anyway. It's a starter soufflé that's perfect served as a lunch alongside a tangy salad.**

PORT
LAND
OREGON
www.jarlsbergusa.com
JARLSBERG

CREPES: SAVORY OR SWEET

MAKES TWENTY-FOUR 1-OUNCE CREPES

Here's a little secret: I've had one thing in my pocket on every single cooking competition I've ever been on. It's an index card with a crepe batter recipe on it. It may come as a surprise, but I know that if I have a crepe batter recipe I can always make something special, because a good crepe is always impressive. Unlike American-style pancakes, which are supposed to be thick and fluffy, crepes are meant to be thin and pliable. They're the casing for an array of savory or sweet fillings.

The process of making the crepe batter is very similar to making standard pancake batter, but the ratio of ingredients makes for a thinner, smoother batter. And the key is in not using too much batter for each crepe—you'll need far less to coat the bottom of the pan than you think. And one more thing: don't feel bad when your first three or four crepes don't work out. As any classically trained chef will agree, the first few are always slightly imperfect—great for snacking and checking for seasoning.

5 large eggs

1 cup milk

½ cup all-purpose flour

¼ teaspoon kosher salt

¾ cup (1½ sticks) unsalted butter, for the pan

Savory or sweet filling (see page 228)

PREP: CRACK THE EGGS INTO A MEASURING CUP OR SMALL BOWL

1. In a large bowl, whisk together the eggs and milk. Add the flour and salt and whisk again until the batter is smooth.
2. Let the batter rest at room temperature for 30 minutes.
3. Heat a small or medium nonstick pan over medium heat. Or, if you happen to have a crepe pan, use that. Nonstick is the important thing.

{ CONTINUED }

Melt a small pat of the butter in the pan, swirling it around to coat the bottom evenly.

4. Working with a liquid measuring cup or using a 2-ounce ladle, add 2 ounces (¼ cup) of the batter to the pan. Lift the pan by the handle and swirl it in a circular motion to spread the batter thinly and evenly. Cook until the batter sets, about 1 minute, then loosen the sides with a rubber spatula and use the spatula to flip the crepe. Cook for 30 seconds on the other side, then transfer the crepe to a plate.

5. Evenly spread the filling of your choice across the surface of the crepe. Fold it in half and then in half again, creating a triangle.

6. Repeat to make the rest of the crepes, using more butter as needed before adding the batter to the pan.

SAVORY FILLINGS

Grated Gruyère cheese with Caramelized Onions (page 7)

Oven-Roasted Tomatoes (page 12)

Herb Pesto (page 36) with fresh mozzarella

Braised duck meat from the Winter Duck Leg Braise (page 167)

SWEET FILLINGS

Butter and sugar

Lemon Curd (page 271) with fresh raspberries

Caramel

Chocolate ganache

Peanut butter and jelly

Freshly whipped cream and sliced fresh strawberries

POACHED ARCTIC CHAR

MAKES **4** SERVINGS

As into modern cooking as I am, I still love the classics, and poaching salmon is as classically French as it gets. If done right, poaching is my favorite way to eat salmon; its slight fattiness helps it stand up to a poach without drying out. But I've had poached salmon a thousand times, so I wanted to explore the same technique on a different fish. I knew I'd need one with similar properties, which led me to arctic char. If you've never had the pleasure of eating arctic char, here's your opportunity. Related to both salmon and trout, it has the same distinctive orange-red flesh and fattiness of salmon, but it's like a trout in that it's smaller. Its flavor is cleaner than that of salmon but also richer than trout's. It's kind of the best of both worlds—both delicious and environmentally sustainable!

½ lemon, sliced into thin wheels

1 tablespoon whole black peppercorns

2 bay leaves

¼ cup dry white wine

1 teaspoon kosher salt

4 (5-ounce) skin-on arctic char fillets or steaks

PREP: SLICE THE LEMON

1. In a high-sided sauté pan or shallow saucepan, combine all the ingredients except for the fish. Add 8 cups water and bring the poaching liquid to a boil over high heat.
2. Turn down the heat to maintain a simmer and gently add the fish fillets to the liquid.
3. Turn the heat even lower, until the liquid calms down to a very gentle simmer, only occasionally bubbling. Continue to cook until the fish is done, 8 to 12 minutes, depending on the thickness of the fillets. You can sneak a peek by flaking a small bit of the flesh—if it's opaque in the center, it's done. If it's still red, it needs another minute or two.

{ CONTINUED }

4. Use a slotted spatula or spoon to gently remove the fillets from the poaching liquid.

5. The fish can be eaten naked, without a sauce, because the poaching liquid will have infused so much great flavor. I love the simplicity of eating the fish in this way, maybe accompanied only by a side salad.

* If you want to serve the fish alongside a sauce, try Curry Golden Raisin Sauce (page 54) or All-Around Mustard Sauce (page 47).

* This fish will taste delicious the next day, chilled from a rest in the refrigerator and eaten for brunch with Cucumber, Dill, and Yogurt Salad (page 96).

ARANCINE

MAKES TWENTY 2-INCH RICE BALLS

Risotto? Deep-frying? These are two potentially intimidating concepts for the home cook, but after you've made this recipe once, it will join your comfort-food repertoire for sure. You'll have to get your hands a bit dirty when shaping the rice balls, which makes it a good one for enlisting the kids' help. But not to worry—the crispy outside and warm, gooey inside make these arancine well worth the not-so-hard work.

1 cup Arborio rice

4 cups Chicken Stock (page 27)

5 large eggs

½ cup grated Parmesan cheese

3 thin slices of ham, diced (¼ cup)

2 cups seasoned bread crumbs

½ teaspoon kosher salt

¼ teaspoon freshly cracked black pepper

2 quarts canola oil, for frying

¾ cup diced fresh mozzarella (about 3 ounces)

PREP: SEPARATE 2 OF THE EGGS, RESERVING 2 WHITES AND 1 YOLK SEPARATELY (DISCARD THE REMAINING YOLK) • GRATE THE PARMESAN • DICE THE HAM • DICE THE MOZZARELLA

1. Use the method on page 3 to make al dente risotto with the rice and chicken stock.

2. Transfer the rice to a baking sheet or large baking dish and let cool to room temperature. Add the 2 egg whites and 1 egg yolk, the Parmesan, ham, and 1 cup of the bread crumbs. Season with the salt and pepper and mix to blend well.

3. In a deep fryer, heat the canola oil to 350°F. If you don't have a deep fryer, use a heavy-bottomed Dutch oven with a frying thermometer clipped to the side. Take care to fill the pot no more than two-thirds full of oil, as the oil is a fire hazard if it boils over.

{ CONTINUED }

4. Using your clean hands, form some of the rice mixture into a small ball about the size of a golf ball and press a deep thumbprint into the center. Fill the center with a few cubes of mozzarella and re-form, encasing the cheese inside the rice. Repeat to make the rest of the rice balls.

5. In a medium bowl, thoroughly beat the remaining 3 whole eggs. Place the remaining 1 cup bread crumbs in another bowl. Coat a rice ball in the beaten eggs, then dredge it in the bread crumbs to cover completely. Set the rice ball on a plate and repeat with the remaining rice balls until they're all breaded.

6. Working in batches, fry the arancine in the hot oil until golden brown, 5 to 6 minutes. Don't crowd the arancine in the fryer.

7. Transfer the arancine to paper towels to drain and serve immediately.

*** You can buy good-quality seasoned bread crumbs, or you can make your own by mixing bread crumbs with dried or chopped fresh parsley, oregano, salt, cracked black pepper, and even a pinch of chili flakes.**

CRISPY SPAETZLE WITH ROASTED SUNCHOKES

MAKES 4 SIDE SERVINGS

Sometimes the Fear Factor lies in the unknown or the exotic. Foreign or unusual ingredients or dishes can be tricky to tackle if you aren't familiar with the taste, texture, desired result, or even pronunciation! This spaetzle and sunchoke dish is a good way to dip your toe into new waters. Spaetzle, pronounced *shpet*-zul, is a German-style noodle or dumpling not too dissimilar to egg noodles or pasta. It takes on the flavors of its sauce or seasonings, so it's a nice blank canvas to work with. Sunchokes have a fairly subtle yet distinctive flavor—give them a try and see what you think!

SPAETZLE

- 1 cup all-purpose flour
- ½ teaspoon plus 2 tablespoons kosher salt
- ⅛ teaspoon freshly grated nutmeg
- 2 large eggs
- ¼ cup milk
- 2 tablespoons extra-virgin olive oil

ROASTED SUNCHOKES

- 3 tablespoons unsalted butter
- 1 cup (5 small) ¼-inch-diced unpeeled sunchokes
- 1 teaspoon chopped fresh rosemary
- 2 garlic cloves, chopped
- 2 tablespoons chopped fresh parsley

PREP: SCRUB AND DICE THE SUNCHOKES • CHOP THE ROSEMARY AND PARSLEY • PEEL AND CHOP THE GARLIC

Salting the water well is really important for the final flavor of the spaetzle.

1. To make the spaetzle, combine the flour, ½ teaspoon of the salt, and the nutmeg in a medium bowl and make a well in the center of the mixture.
2. In a separate bowl, whisk together the eggs and milk. Pour the mixture into the well in the flour and use a fork to combine the wet and dry ingredients. Stir until smooth, cover with plastic wrap, and let rest in the fridge, for 30 minutes.
3. Bring a gallon of water to a rolling boil and season with the remaining 2 tablespoons salt.

{ CONTINUED }

4. Place a colander or long perforated spatula or spaetzle maker over the water and press some of the spaetzle dough through the holes with a large spoon, letting the batter fall in long "noodles" through the perforations into the water. Repeat with the rest of the dough, working fairly quickly so that the spaetzle finish cooking at the same time.

5. When the spaetzle float, strain them through a colander as you would pasta and toss into a bowl with the olive oil. Gently mix to make sure the spaetzle don't stick together. Set aside while you prepare the sunchokes.

6. To make the sunchokes, in a large sauté pan over medium-high heat, melt 2 tablespoons of the butter. When the butter is sizzling, add the sunchokes and cook until they're browned, 2 to 3 minutes. Add the rosemary and garlic and cook until fragrant.

7. Add the remaining 1 tablespoon butter and let it foam in the pan, then add the spaetzle to the herbed butter. Cook the spaetzle over medium-high heat until they start to crisp, turning a beautiful toasted brown color.

8. Just before serving, stir in the parsley.

* This is delectable as a side dish. For a more substantial main course, top it with braised duck (page 167), pulled pork (page 159), or slow-braised beef (page 152) from the "Low and Slow" chapter, or with a simple sprinkle of Parmesan cheese.

* Sunchokes are also called Jerusalem artichokes, although they're not artichokes at all. Their rhizome shape can make them look like ginger or fresh turmeric, but they're actually related to sunflowers. In the Northeast, you can find sunchokes in specialty stores and markets in the fall.

* If you want to experiment with spaetzle and can't find sunchokes, substitute two or three large portobello mushrooms. Just take care to sauté the chopped mushrooms until they're dry in the pan—the liquid will keep your spaetzle from getting crispy.

EASY COQ AU VIN

MAKES 4 TO 6 SERVINGS

As with many people, the first time I ever laid eyes on or heard of coq au vin was watching Julia Child on television and reading her cookbooks, which are more like cooking bibles. Watching her make what seemed to be incredibly intimidating classical dishes, like coq au vin, motivated me to attempt them, even though I was scared and honestly, half the time, never thought they would work out. Diving headfirst into those recipes made me realize I could use my basic knowledge of a few culinary techniques to pull together a dish that I thought only Julia Child could make. Believe me, growing up and learning how to cook, I had lots of failed dishes, but every dish was a success because I came away having learned something that made me the chef I am today.

- 6 slices smoked bacon, diced
- 1 Spanish onion, cut into wedges
- 2 cups button mushrooms, quartered
- 2 tablespoons unsalted butter
- ¼ cup all-purpose flour
- 1 (750 ml) bottle red wine
- 2 tablespoons olive oil
- 6 bone-in, skin-on chicken legs
- 3 cups Chicken Stock (page 27) or store-bought low-sodium chicken stock
- 2 teaspoons kosher salt
- ¼ teaspoon freshly cracked black pepper
- 2 tablespoons minced fresh chives

PREP: DICE THE BACON • PEEL AND CUT THE ONION • QUARTER THE MUSHROOMS • MINCE THE CHIVES

1. In a Dutch oven over medium heat, cook the bacon until it's crisp and all the fat is rendered.

2. Add the onion and cook for 2 minutes, then add the mushrooms. Cook until the vegetables release some of their natural juices, using a wooden spoon to scrape up the delicious bacon renderings.

{ CONTINUED }

3. Add the butter and let it melt, then sprinkle in the flour. Stir and cook the mixture for 3 minutes to make sure the flour is cooked out, preventing any raw flour taste in the sauce.

4. Add the wine and stir or whisk vigorously until the mixture has no flour clumps. Bring to a boil, then turn down the heat to maintain a simmer and cook until the wine has reduced by half, 6 to 8 minutes.

5. Meanwhile, heat the olive oil in a large sauté pan over high heat. When the oil is hot, add the chicken legs, skin side down. You should hear a distinct sizzle when each leg is added. Add only as many legs as you can sear comfortably in the pan; you might have to work in two batches. Cook the legs on the skin side for 3 minutes, or until nicely browned, then flip and cook for just 1 minute on the other side.

6. Transfer all the legs to the Dutch oven with the vegetables and wine.

7. Deglaze the sauté pan with 1 cup of stock, scraping the bottom of the pan with a wooden spoon to get all the flavorful bits. Cook for 1 minute, leaving no flavor behind! Pour the remaining 2 cups of stock in with the chicken and veggies.

8. Simmer over medium-low heat, covered, for about 1 hour, or until the chicken meat is just about to fall off the bone.

9. Serve the chicken legs over rice or noodles with a generous ladle of the rich sauce. Top with minced chives.

*** I call this "Easy Coq au Vin" because I've eliminated the usual overnight marinating time and call for chicken legs rather than a whole laying hen or a rooster, which are generally hard to find at American butchers. And although you could certainly make coq au vin with a regular chicken, who has room in their fridge for a whole chicken submerged in a big container of red wine for twenty-four hours?**

HERB-STUFFED WHOLE FISH

MAKES 4 SERVINGS

Just like any meat, fish has the most flavor when prepared skin-on and bone-in. When I started cooking Italian cuisine, whole fish were on the menu time and time again, and my eyes and my taste buds were happy to embrace it. This recipe seemed a good candidate as one "most likely to scare" because, well, whole fish are intimidating. But just ask your fish guy or gal to clean and gut the fish for you, and most of the hard work is done. And while you're at it, have a chat about which types and size of fish work the best for cooking whole—don't be shy! They're the experts, after all, and are usually happy to offer advice.

For your first attempt, choose a flaky, white-fleshed fish that weighs about 14 ounces. You can also cook sardines on the bone, but I don't recommend an oily fish such as bluefish, mackerel, or arctic char. After a few attempts, this dish will no doubt give you a sense of pride and satisfaction—it always looks like a work of art in the end. Pat yourself on the back.

- 4 branzino or dorade, scaled and gutted (look for 12- to 14-ounce fish)
- Kosher salt and freshly cracked black pepper
- 2 lemons, cut crosswise into paper-thin rounds
- 1 bunch fresh thyme
- 1 bunch fresh oregano
- ½ bunch fresh flat-leaf parsley
- ¼ cup olive oil

PREP: GATHER FOUR 12-INCH SKEWERS • CLEAN AND SLICE THE LEMONS

Your roasting pan must be screaming hot before you add the stuffed fish.

1. Preheat the oven to 475°F.
2. Place a large oven-safe sauté pan or baking sheet on the lower rack of the oven to preheat.
3. Season the belly cavity of the fish with salt and pepper.
4. Place 2 or 3 lemon slices and a few sprigs of thyme, oregano, and parsley into the cavity of each fish. Really, just fill the cavities with all the herbs and lemon that will fit.

{ CONTINUED }

5. Now for the fun part! Close the cavity of each fish by "sewing" a skewer through the skin. Hold the skin together, tucking in the herbs, and weave the skewer up and down through the skin to seal the cavity. The skewer stays in while the fish is cooked.

6. Season the outside of the fish with a generous amount of salt and pepper. Divide the olive oil among the four fish and use your fingers to rub it on, coating them well on all sides.

7. Carefully remove the preheated pan from the oven and gently place the fish in it. There should be a searing noise—that means you're doing it right! Return the pan to the oven and roast the fish for 10 minutes.

8. Remove the pan from the oven and use a thin spatula to gently turn each fish over. Return the pan to the oven and roast the fish for 10 minutes more. The skin should be nice and crispy on both sides.

9. Remove the fish from the oven and let rest for 2 minutes. Carefully remove the skewers and place the fish (herbs and all) on a large plate for serving. Since these are whole fish, be mindful of the bones as you eat, and advise your guests to be careful as well.

* **Ask your fishmonger to thoroughly clean the fish so that all you have to do once you get home is season and roast it. Many people know they can ask their butcher to cut meat to their specifications, but most folks don't ask the same of their fishmonger. Whether you're buying whole fish or fillets, you can ask him or her to remove skin, bones, and scales and to portion and clean your fish just as you need it for any given recipe.**

* **You can modify the recipe by buying fillets, seasoning them, and searing them on the stovetop for a minute or two to get the skin crispy. Then top the fillets with lemon slices, herbs, and a drizzle of olive oil and bake them in a preheated oven. Depending on the thickness of the fillets, this should take only 6 to 7 minutes. When the fish is flaky and opaque, it's done.**

* **Garnish the platter of herb-stuffed fish with Mediterranean Potato Salad (page 198).**

SCALLOP "CEVICHE"

MAKES 4 TO 6 SERVINGS

Traditionally, ceviche is raw fish that's marinated in a combination of citrus juices and spices that cure it, effectively cooking the fish while they infuse huge flavor. Unsure of when the raw fish is cured enough to be safe, many people leave ceviche to the professionals. This is my version of ceviche, which actually falls somewhere between a ceviche and an escabeche, in which the fish is cooked and then marinated. It's a little less scary, but I also prefer the texture when the scallops are poached briefly before they're marinated.

- Zest of 2 lemons
- 3 tablespoons fresh lemon juice (from 1 lemon)
- Zest of 1 lime
- 1 tablespoon fresh lime juice (from 1 lime)
- 2 scallions, thinly sliced
- 2 shallots, thinly sliced
- ⅓ cup olive oil
- 1 tablespoon chopped fresh cilantro
- 1 tablespoon chopped fresh parsley
- 1 red bell pepper, julienned
- 1 tomato, diced
- 1 tablespoon sherry vinegar
- 1 teaspoon kosher salt, plus more for the poaching water
- ¼ cup Sweet and Spicy Chili Oil (page 38)
- 1 pound scallops

Sea or bay scallops both work fine.

PREP: ZEST AND JUICE THE LEMONS AND LIME • SLICE THE SCALLIONS • PEEL AND SLICE THE SHALLOTS • CHOP THE CILANTRO AND PARSLEY • SEED AND JULIENNE THE PEPPER • DICE THE TOMATO

1. In a large bowl, combine all the ingredients except the scallops. Whisk and set aside to let the flavors develop.

2. Bring a large pot of salted water to a boil. Poach the scallops in the boiling water for 1 minute.

3. Drain the scallops and add them directly to the marinade. Marinate in the fridge for just 30 minutes before serving. (If you overmarinate the scallops, they'll become tough and rubbery.)

* For more tips and advice about working with scallops, see Seared Scallops (page 221).

* You could absolutely substitute shrimp, squid, or any white fish in this recipe. You can also play with the flavors by using Meyer lemon, grapefruit, orange, passion fruit, or even pomegranate in place of the lemon and lime.

DUCK BREAST WITH PINE NUT RELISH

MAKES 4 SERVINGS

Duck breast may not be at the top of your weeknight dinner recipe roster, but it totally should be! Chicken seems to be everyone's go-to weeknight protein, but duck breast is even more foolproof to work with because it comes with a built-in ingredient that almost guarantees a moist, juicy, flavorful dish: duck fat! It renders and naturally bastes the duck, leaving a crackly, crispy skin behind. You can help it along by carefully spooning some of the rendered fat over the breast as it cooks. Or add a sprig of rosemary or thyme to the butter for an added layer of flavor.

And the duck fat isn't done working for you once the breasts are cooked. Save it in the fridge and lend extra special flavor to roasted potatoes, sautéed veggies, or steak fries later in the week!

- 2 cups white balsamic vinegar
- ½ cup pine nuts, toasted
- 3 large sage leaves, cut into chiffonade
- ⅛ teaspoon cayenne pepper
- Kosher salt
- 4 duck breasts
- ½ teaspoon freshly cracked black pepper
- 2 tablespoons unsalted butter

PREP: TOAST THE PINE NUTS IN A SMALL SAUTÉ PAN OVER LOW HEAT UNTIL FRAGRANT • CHIFFONADE THE SAGE LEAVES

1. In a high-sided sauté pan over high heat, simmer the white balsamic vinegar until it has reduced to ¼ cup, about 20 minutes. It should be golden in color and resemble syrup. Remove from the heat.

2. In a small bowl, combine the pine nuts, sage, and cayenne. Pour the reduced vinegar over the nuts and stir to combine. Season with salt to taste and set aside.

{ CONTINUED }

3. Preheat the oven to 400°F.

4. Using a sharp knife, score the duck fat very lightly in a crosshatch marking. This looks great and ensures a really crispy skin. Generously season both sides of each breast with salt and black pepper.

5. Heat a large oven-safe sauté pan over medium heat. Add all the duck breasts, skin side down. Cook until the skin is crispy, 12 to 15 minutes, using a ladle occasionally to remove some of the excess fat (reserve it in a bowl for later use).

6. Use tongs to turn the breasts over. Place the pan in the oven and cook the duck for 10 to 12 minutes, until medium or medium-well, your preference.

7. Let the duck breasts rest for a few minutes while you finish the pine nut relish.

8. Melt the butter in a sauté pan over medium-low heat until golden brown. Remove from the heat and stir in the pine nut mixture. Let it sit until it's combined.

9. Slice the duck breast and serve topped with the pine nut relish.

* **Keep a measuring cup or glass jar next to the pan as you cook the duck. The duck will give off so much fat that you'll almost always have to ladle some out of the pan as the duck cooks. Transfer the leftover duck fat to a small mason jar or Tupperware with a lid and refrigerate it for later use.**

* **Serve the seared duck breasts over blanched broccoli rabe or asparagus (see the blanching procedure on page 9).**

FOR YOUR SWEET TOOTH

Eight chapters in, perhaps you're confident and flexible enough to have thrown away your measuring cups and spoons, putting your own twist on dishes and using recipes only as guidelines. But even if you're liberated from the rigidity of recipes in your regular cooking, you need to break out those measuring cups and spoons again—it's pastry time!

Savory chefs complain so much about having to make desserts. In televised cooking competitions, dessert is the dreaded task that nobody wants. Chefs so often crumble when it comes to this round—and for good reason. When we go to culinary school, we have to make a choice between culinary arts or pastry, because pastry is its own art and science. Pastry chefs spend years honing their craft, in whatever direction they go—pastry, chocolate, wedding cakes, bread—whether their journey starts in culinary school or through work in patisseries or bakeries or restaurants. And dessert is powerful, giving diners the last and, often, lasting impression of a restaurant. However delicious and beautifully plated those appetizers and entrées were, a diner's overall experience is tarnished when dessert hits a low note. The same is true at home.

Having a smattering of trusty and reliable dessert recipes is worth it, and you're at an advantage if (unlike me) you're naturally inclined to follow a recipe. Correct ratios of leavening agents and flours are necessary to ensure light-as-air cakes and cookies. Just the right amount of sugar is required for a perfectly sweet balance in your creamy panna cotta or ice cream or pie filling. And while we can freely substitute many meats and veggies and herbs and spices in savory cooking, even a simple swap of dark chocolate for milk chocolate in a chocolate mousse can throw it off because of the different amounts of sugar and fat in the chocolates. So, even if you've managed well enough with the other recipes in this book by eyeballing your quantities, it's important to be accurate with measurements in this chapter.

For Your Sweet Tooth

ANGEL FOOD CAKE

MAKES ONE 10-INCH CAKE

When I started culinary school, one of my biggest fans was my dad. He was one of the only people in my family who respected the culinary arts and understood why I would want to make it my career. Around the same time, he started taking amateur classes in baking and pastry. Being patient and meticulous, he relished the discipline of pastry. He loved the exact measuring and the science behind it—almost the complete opposite of me. This angel food cake is one of his favorite sweet recipes, maybe because it involves so many precise pastry techniques and skills—whipping egg whites, folding, measuring, patience—and it even requires a specialty pan! Angel food cake is really a very technical dessert masquerading as a simple one. When I find myself trying to speed through this recipe, I hear my dad's patient voice in my head: *Take it easy, Amanda.* Each time I make this cake, I am honoring him.

1 cup cake flour

½ teaspoon baking powder

1 cup confectioners' sugar

1 cup granulated sugar

1½ cups egg whites (from about 12 eggs)

1 tablespoon warm water

1½ teaspoons cream of tartar

½ teaspoon kosher salt

1½ teaspoons pure vanilla extract

½ teaspoon almond extract

PREP: SEPARATE THE EGGS, RESERVING THE WHITES AND DISCARDING THE YOLKS OR SAVING THEM FOR ANOTHER RECIPE

Save the yolks to make shortbread cookies, page 271.

1. Preheat the oven to 350°F.
2. Sift together the cake flour and baking powder onto waxed paper and set aside.
3. Combine the confectioners' sugar and granulated sugar in a small bowl and set aside.
4. Place the egg whites and warm water in the clean bowl of a stand mixer fitted with the whisk attachment. Beat on medium speed until frothy.

{ CONTINUED }

5. Add the cream of tartar, salt, vanilla, and almond extract. Increase the speed to medium-high and continue beating until the whites form soft peaks.

6. Turn down the speed to low and add the sugar mixture 1 tablespoon at a time. Stop the machine, making sure the sugar is blended well by scraping down the sides of the bowl with a rubber spatula. Turn the machine back on and beat for 30 seconds more.

If using a Bundt pan, spray the inside with cooking spray to make sure the cake doesn't stick!

7. Carefully scrape the meringue into a large bowl. Add the sifted flour mix in three parts, rotating the bowl after each addition, gently pulling the egg whites up from the bottom and folding over until the flour is incorporated. Take care not to overmix, and never stir the batter or it will deflate.

8. Gently pour the batter into an angel food cake or Bundt pan and smooth it lightly with the back of a spatula.

9. Bake for 30 to 35 minutes, or until a cake tester or long skewer inserted into the center comes out clean.

10. To cool, turn the pan upside down onto a cooling rack. Most angel food cake pans have "feet" at the top that support the pan while inverted to help the cake cool faster. When the cake is cool, a removable bottom makes it a breeze to release the cake.

* Serve with fresh seasonal berries or even Grape Compote (page 267). A dollop of lightly sweetened fresh whipped cream wouldn't go amiss either.

DEEP-DISH APPLE-RHUBARB PIE

MAKES ONE 10-INCH DEEP-DISH DOUBLE-CRUSTED PIE

Pie is a surefire crowd-pleaser, and the crust is always the best part. So what's better than a pie with one crust? A pie with two crusts! A great pie dough recipe is an ace in the hole when you're in need of a dessert for nearly any occasion—a potluck, a dinner party, or even *The Next Iron Chef*! For many years I didn't have a rolling pin in my teeny home kitchen, so I wrapped a bottle of wine or olive oil in plastic wrap and used that! It really works—just make sure it hasn't been opened . . .

PIE DOUGH

4¼ cups all-purpose flour, plus ½ cup for dusting

1 tablespoon granulated sugar

1 teaspoon kosher salt

1 cup (2 sticks) unsalted butter, very cold

4 large eggs

PIE FILLING

8 Gala or Granny Smith apples, peeled, cored, and cut into ¼-inch slices

4 rhubarb stalks, cut into ¼-inch half-moons

1 teaspoon ground cinnamon

¼ cup granulated sugar

Juice of 2 lemons

3 tablespoons graham cracker crumbs (from about 1 cracker)

5 teaspoons all-purpose flour

Nonstick cooking spray, for the pie pan

2 large eggs, for the egg wash

¼ cup turbinado sugar (Sugar in the Raw) or granulated sugar, for sprinkling

PREP: PEEL, CORE, AND SLICE THE APPLES • SLICE THE RHUBARB • JUICE THE LEMONS • CRUSH THE GRAHAM CRACKER INTO CRUMBS • CLEAN A LARGE, CLEAR SURFACE FOR ROLLING OUT THE DOUGH

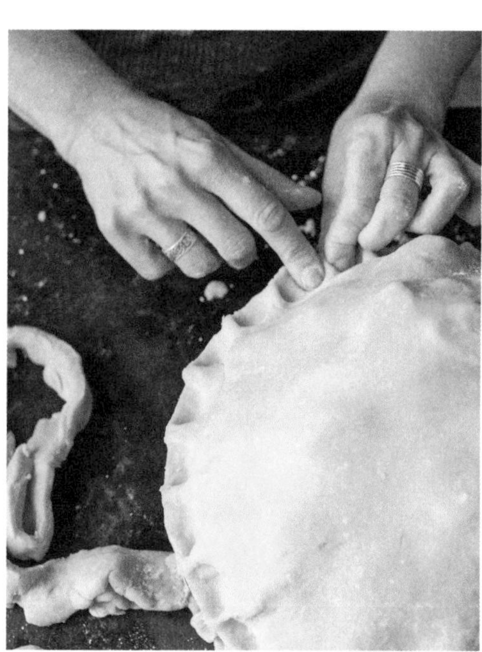

1. To make the pie dough, in a large bowl, mix the flour, sugar, and salt. With a pastry blender or your fingers, cut in the cold butter until the mixture is in pea-size pieces.

2. In a separate bowl, beat the eggs with a fork until fluffy and pale yellow.

{ CONTINUED }

3. Add the eggs to the flour mixture and mix with a fork until the dough just comes together. Use your clean hands to form it into a ball, taking care not to overwork the dough.

4. Cut the ball in half, forming two smaller balls of dough. Gently press down on each to form two disks. Wrap each disk in plastic wrap and refrigerate them for at least 2 hours, or even overnight.

5. When the dough has chilled sufficiently, make the pie filling. In a large bowl, combine all the filling ingredients. Stir to make sure the flour and sugar combine and start to melt onto the fruit.

6. Preheat the oven to 375°F. Coat a 10-inch deep-dish pie pan with cooking spray.

7. Remove the plastic wrap from the dough disks and place them on a lightly floured surface. Using a rolling pin, roll one disk into a ¼-inch-thick circle that's about 2 inches wider than the pie pan.

8. Roll the dough circle onto the rolling pin. Lift the dough over the pie dish and slowly release it from the rolling pin, letting the dough drape over the pan as it unfurls. The dough should be centered over the pan and hanging evenly over the edge. Do *not* trim the crust yet!

9. Spoon the fruit filling into the center of the crust, creating a mountain of fruit with a high central point. With clean hands, gently push down on the center point to even out the filling into a heaping mound and gently press the crust into the sides of the pan. Trim the crust right to the edge all the way around the pie pan.

10. Roll out the top crust the same way and drape it over the fruit filling, letting the excess dough hang over the sides of the pie pan.

11. Flute the edges by pinching the dough between your thumb and forefinger all the way around the edge. Trim any excess dough that hangs over after fluting around the edges. Cut small decorative/functional holes or slits in the top crust with a paring knife or a fork to allow steam to escape.

12. Lightly whisk the eggs in a small bowl with a fork to make the egg wash. Brush the crust with the egg wash with a pastry brush or your fingers. Sprinkle turbinado sugar all over the crust.

13. Place the pie pan on a baking sheet and bake for about 1 hour, or until the crust is golden brown and the juices begin to bubble.

14. Let the pie sit at room temperature for a few hours before cutting; this will allow the fruit filling to firm up, if you can wait that long!

---

* **Aluminum and ceramic pie pans are better conductors of heat. Steer clear of glass pie dishes.**

* **Mix in any other fruit of your choice, such as a plum or pear or blueberries, if rhubarb is unavailable. Berries give off more liquid, so increase the flour by 2 teaspoons.**

* **Don't be afraid to be generous with the pie filling—the fruit will cook down.**

* **A small brand-new paintbrush can work as a pastry brush.**

SUMMER BERRY FRUIT CRUMBLE

MAKES 4 TO 6 SERVINGS

This was one of the first desserts I made when I was learning how to cook, and I was so proud of it. In the summer, when berries are in abundance, it's so much fun to make—and so easy! No special equipment is needed—you could practically make it with your bare hands. In the fall, when berries are out of season, this recipe works great with peeled, sliced apples and pears.

CRUMBLE TOPPING

1¾ cups all-purpose flour

1 cup packed light brown sugar

Pinch of kosher salt

¾ cup (1½ sticks) unsalted butter, cold, cut into small pieces

FRUIT FILLING

4 cups strawberries, hulled and quartered

1 cup blueberries

Zest of 1 lemon

2 tablespoons cornstarch

2 tablespoons all-purpose flour

PREP: HULL AND QUARTER THE STRAWBERRIES • ZEST THE LEMON

1. Preheat the oven to 375°F.
2. To make the crumble topping, combine the flour, sugar, and salt in a medium bowl. Use your clean hands to rub the butter into the flour until the mixture is in chickpea-size lumps. Set aside.
3. To make the filling, combine the filling ingredients in a 10-inch pie pan or 9 × 9-inch baking dish and mix gently but well. Use a spatula or the back of a wooden spoon to flatten the fruit into an even surface.
4. Sprinkle the crumble mixture over the fruit, covering every nook and cranny as best you can.
5. Bake for about 25 minutes, or until the fruit starts to bubble over the crumble and the crumble is lightly browned.
6. Serve warm or slightly cooled.

Serve with whipped cream or ice cream!

COCONUT MACAROONS

MAKES 24 COOKIES

I've always been a lover of coconut. My favorite birthday cake is a layered coconut cake, seemingly sky-high with layers and coconut shavings. These cookies are packed with texture and flavor to satisfy any coconut lover. It gets the job done when I'm craving all that coconut and it's not my birthday!

Nonstick cooking spray

4 cups sweetened shredded coconut

⅔ cup sweetened condensed milk

½ teaspoon pure vanilla extract

⅛ teaspoon kosher salt

2 egg whites

PREP: SEPARATE THE EGGS, RESERVING THE WHITES AND DISCARDING THE YOLKS OR SAVING THEM FOR ANOTHER USE

1. Preheat the oven to 375°F. Grease a baking sheet using nonstick cooking spray or line with parchment paper.
2. In a medium bowl, mix together the coconut, condensed milk, vanilla, and salt.
3. In a separate clean bowl, using a whisk or a hand mixer, whip the egg whites until they're white and glossy.
4. Gently fold the egg whites into the coconut mixture.
5. Using a large spoon or cookie scoop, make 1½-tablespoon mounds of the batter and drop them onto the prepared baking sheet, keeping them 1 inch apart.
6. Bake for 20 minutes, or until golden brown, rotating the baking sheet after about 10 minutes of cooking. You want them dried on the outside but with a chewy center.
7. Set the macaroons aside to cool completely. Store them in an airtight container and these delicious treats will last up to 5 days—if they don't get eaten before that!

* As I'm a believer in efficiency, it's always nice to satisfy your coconut and chocolate cravings at the same time. After the cookies are baked and cooled, dip half of each cookie in melted dark chocolate.

IMPRESSIVE DARK CHOCOLATE MOUSSE

MAKES 4 SERVINGS

It's no secret to my friends and fans of *Chopped* that I'm a chocoholic! In my opinion, if you have chocolate in your dessert, the meal is officially complete. Chocolate mousse has always been a favorite of mine—it's basically chocolate pudding for adults. It's so easy to make, yet you can also dress it up to impress your guests. Serve it in a delicate glass and add berries, a cookie, or a wafer for an elegant finish to even a modest weeknight meal. This is definitely my go-to crowd-pleaser, and it's tailor-made for a tiny home kitchen. You don't even need to turn on the oven!

- 8 ounces dark chocolate (70% cacao or higher), chopped
- 4 ounces milk chocolate, chopped
- 3 egg whites
- 2½ cups heavy cream
- ¼ cup confectioners' sugar
- ⅛ teaspoon kosher salt

PREP: CHOP THE CHOCOLATES • SEPARATE THE EGGS, RESERVING THE WHITES AND DISCARDING THE YOLKS OR SAVING THEM FOR ANOTHER USE

1. Combine the chocolates in a medium stainless-steel or glass bowl.
2. Bring 2 cups water to a simmer over medium-low heat in a saucepan that will hold the bowl without it touching the boiling water. Place the bowl of chocolate over the simmering water to create a double boiler. Let the chocolate melt, stirring occasionally.
3. Turn off the heat and set the bowl on the counter to cool slightly.
4. In the bowl of a stand mixer fitted with the whisk attachment, or with a hand mixer or a regular balloon whisk and lots of muscle, whip the egg whites to soft peaks. Set aside.
5. In a separate bowl, whip the cream with the sugar until it's just starting to thicken.

{ CONTINUED }

Working with chocolate is a beautiful thing, so slow down and enjoy the rich chocolaty aroma that's wafting through your kitchen at this moment.

6. Gently fold the cream mixture into the melted chocolate with a rubber spatula, then gently fold in the beaten egg whites, taking extra care by bringing the chocolate mix from the bottom of the bowl up and over the whites and rotating the bowl while folding. This will ensure a light and fluffy mousse—so don't rush it!

7. Divide the mousse among individual serving dishes and refrigerate for at least 1 hour before serving.

*** You can serve this mousse with fresh whipped cream for additional oomph. To make it even fancier, fold a teaspoon or two of your favorite liqueur into the whipped cream—try raspberry framboise or orangey Grand Marnier, as both raspberry and orange go well with dark chocolate.**

YOGURT PANNA COTTA WITH DRIED CRANBERRY AND GRAPE COMPOTE

MAKES 4 SERVINGS
(5 CUPS PANNA COTTA AND 1½ CUPS COMPOTE)

Panna cotta has saved my life several times! I'm by no means a pastry chef, but I can execute a few desserts really well. When I first opened a restaurant in Brooklyn, I had to be the chef, the pastry chef, and a line cook. I needed to have a fast, easy-to-make dessert that was still impressive enough to serve to all my new customers—and the panna cotta was a hit. I could make it in large quantities and embellish it with seasonal fruits and sauces; it was versatile and made me look as if I had a pastry chef on staff. Many years later at a different restaurant, I found myself in the same position as the executive chef taking over the pastry station . . . *yikes.* My panna cotta went on the menu immediately. About a year later, I was asked to appear on *Martha,* Martha Stewart's talk show, and I created the panna cotta with Greek yogurt for a healthier twist. I topped it with this cranberry and concord grape compote. Martha loved it, and panna cotta saved me again!

COMPOTE

- 1½ pounds red seedless grapes, stemmed
- ½ cup fresh orange juice
- ½ cup apple cider or apple juice
- 1 cup dried cranberries

PANNA COTTA

- 1½ cups whole milk
- 1 cup heavy cream
- ¼ cup confectioners' sugar
- 1 vanilla bean, halved lengthwise and seeds scraped, or ½ teaspoon pure vanilla extract
- 1 (¼-ounce) envelope unflavored gelatin, or 4 gelatin sheets
- 2 cups plain yogurt, preferably Greek-style

{ CONTINUED }

1. To make the compote, combine the grapes, orange juice, and apple cider in a large heavy-bottomed saucepan over medium heat. Cook until the grapes have released most of their juices, about 20 minutes.
2. Add the cranberries and cook over low heat until they start to soften, about 5 minutes. Transfer to a bowl, cover, and refrigerate.
3. To make the panna cotta, in a small saucepan, mix the milk, cream, sugar, and vanilla and bring to a simmer over low heat. Add the powdered gelatin and whisk until it has dissolved.
4. Transfer the mixture to a large bowl. Add the yogurt and stir until smooth and well combined. Transfer to a spouted measuring cup for easy pouring. Evenly distribute the mixture among four 6-ounce ramekins. Refrigerate until set, at least 2 hours and up to overnight. Serve the panna cotta cold with a dollop of the delicious compote on top.

---

* **Gelatin is a bit temperamental, and if you don't treat it just right, it refuses to work for you. When you dissolve powdered gelatin, it must be heated or it will clump and not melt. While gelatin powder is the most readily available, I recommend gelatin sheets if you can find them because they're easier to work with. Gelatin sheets must be soaked first in cold water until soft, then squeezed to remove all excess water. Unlike powdered gelatin, gelatin sheets should not be heated, so before you combine them with the milk and sugar mixture, first remove it from the heat.**

* **Experiment with different compotes, depending on what types of fruit are fresh and delicious at your local market. Any berry or even stone fruit would work well. And play with herbs in your dessert! A bit of fresh mint, tarragon, basil, or even thyme cooked into the compote will elevate it and leave your guests impressed.**

SHORTBREAD COOKIES WITH LEMON CURD

MAKES TWENTY-FOUR 1-INCH SQUARE COOKIES

One day I was craving chips and dip (as always) but also something sweet, and I had an epiphany. This recipe was the result. It's kind of like a dessert version of chips and dip—buttery shortbread cookies dipped into tangy lemon curd. Heaven—and delicious fun for entertaining.

LEMON CURD

- 4 tablespoons (½ stick) unsalted butter
- 6 tablespoons fresh lemon juice (from 2 to 3 lemons)
- 6 tablespoons granulated sugar
- 4 egg yolks

SHORTBREAD COOKIES

- 10 tablespoons (1 stick plus 2 tablespoons) unsalted butter, at room temperature
- ¼ cup confectioners' sugar
- 1½ tablespoons granulated sugar
- 1½ cups all-purpose flour
- ¼ teaspoon kosher salt

PREP: JUICE THE LEMONS • SEPARATE THE EGGS, RESERVING THE YOLKS AND DISCARDING THE WHITES OR SAVING THEM FOR ANOTHER USE

1. To make the lemon curd, in a small saucepan (not aluminum) over low heat, melt the butter with the lemon juice. Add the granulated sugar and whisk until it has completely dissolved.

2. Remove the pan from the heat and add the egg yolks, one at a time, whisking vigorously as you add them. The combination of whisking and adding the eggs slowly will help to temper the eggs, preventing them from scrambling.

3. Once all of the yolks have been incorporated, place the pan back on the heat and cook until thickened, approximately 3 to 4 minutes.

{ CONTINUED }

4. Strain the curd through a sieve and set aside. (If you're not using the curd right away, cover with plastic and store in the fridge for up to 3 days.)

5. To make the shortbread cookies, preheat the oven to 350°F.

6. In the bowl of a stand mixer fitted with the paddle attachment, beat the butter and sugars together until well combined and fluffy. (Alternatively, you can use a hand mixer.)

7. In a separate bowl, combine the flour and salt. With the stand mixer on low speed, gradually add the flour to the butter-sugar mixture, allowing each addition of the flour to fully mix in before adding more. Turn off the mixer when the dough is fully mixed and has come together.

8. Dump the dough onto a piece of waxed or parchment paper and press it together into a disk. Wrap the dough completely in the paper and refrigerate for 1 hour to chill and rest.

9. Working on the piece of paper or a lightly floured surface, roll out the dough to a roughly ⅓-inch thickness. If the dough is overly soft or sticky, dust it with flour and roll it out between two sheets of parchment or waxed paper.

10. Use a sharp knife to cut the dough into a grid of roughly 1 × 1-inch squares. Reroll any uneven pieces to make more squares.

11. Lay the squares 1 to 2 inches apart on a nonstick baking sheet. Bake for 12 to 15 minutes, or until lightly golden.

12. Serve the cookies with little bowls of lemon curd for dipping.

*** This is a very standard lemon curd recipe, so if you want to experiment with making a lemon curd tart, this would be a great filling!**

*** Warning! Do not use an aluminum saucepan when making the lemon curd—the acid from the lemon juice will react with the aluminum. Use any small stainless-steel, nonstick, or cast-iron saucepan you have on hand.**

COCOA CARROT CAKE WITH CREAM CHEESE ICING

MAKES ONE 10-INCH CAKE, TO SERVE 8

What I love most about putting together these recipes is that they're truly a collection of memories and influences from all the amazing chefs, friends, and cooks who have touched my life. This cake recipe is a gift from my chef friend Gregor Rohlsson, and I made it many times when I worked under him at his restaurant. I fell in love with it because of the richness of the cocoa along with the extra-deep flavor given by the brown sugar and vegetable oil. Try this if you want to push the envelope on your standard carrot cake recipe.

COCOA CARROT CAKE

- Nonstick cooking spray
- 2 cups packed dark brown sugar
- 1½ cups vegetable oil
- 4 large eggs
- 2 teaspoons baking soda
- 1 tablespoon ground cinnamon
- ¾ teaspoon freshly grated nutmeg
- ⅛ teaspoon kosher salt
- ¼ cup unsweetened cocoa powder
- 1¾ cups all-purpose flour
- 1 pound carrots, peeled and coarsely grated
- ½ pound walnuts, chopped

CREAM CHEESE ICING

- 1½ cups (3 sticks) butter, at room temperature
- 1½ pounds cream cheese (three 8-ounce packages), at room temperature
- 3 cups confectioners' sugar
- 1 teaspoon pure vanilla extract

PREP: PEEL AND GRATE THE CARROTS (USE THE GRATER DISK OF A FOOD PROCESSOR, IF YOU HAVE ONE) • CHOP THE WALNUTS

{ CONTINUED }

1. Preheat the oven to 350°F. Line a 10-inch round cake pan with waxed paper. Grease the waxed paper with nonstick cooking spray.
2. In the bowl of a stand mixer fitted with the paddle attachment, or in a bowl with a hand mixer, cream the brown sugar and vegetable oil until fully blended. Add 2 of the eggs and mix them in fully, then add the remaining 2 eggs and mix well.
3. In a medium bowl, combine the baking soda, cinnamon, nutmeg, salt, cocoa, and flour. Slowly incorporate the flour mixture into the sugar-egg mixture, mixing to combine well.
4. Turn off the mixer and use a wooden spoon or rubber spatula to stir the carrots and walnuts into the batter.
5. Pour the batter into the prepared cake pan and bake for 45 minutes to 1 hour, or until a toothpick inserted into the center of the cake comes out clean.
6. Let the cake cool in the pan until cool enough to handle. Run an offset spatula around the inner rim of the pan to loosen the edges of the cake. Place a large piece of waxed paper over the cake. Using the palm of your hand to hold the paper against the cake, carefully flip the cake onto your hand. Carefully flip it back onto a large plate or cake stand to cool further.
7. Meanwhile, make the icing. In a large bowl, use a hand mixer or a wooden spoon to beat the butter and cream cheese together. Add the confectioners' sugar and vanilla and mix until fully incorporated.
8. When the cake is completely cool, use an offset spatula to ice the cake with the cream cheese icing, covering it completely and evenly.
9. Place in the fridge to set for 1 hour. Let the cake come to room temperature just before serving.

*** The best way to ice a cake is really to use a rotating cake stand, but—surprise, surprise—I don't own one! So I improvise and usually place the cake on an inverted cake pan or plate while I ice it. At least it gets it off my counter!**

RICE PUDDING IS THE CURE!

MAKES 4 TO 6 SERVINGS

Rice pudding has always been a comfort food to me. In my home state of New Jersey, it seems that every diner has the same recipe; you can reliably find it doused with cinnamon, with the option to elevate it with a huge "spray" of canned whipped cream. While some might claim chicken soup is the cure, I stand by rice pudding as a cure for whatever ails you. Seriously! I was once very ill with the flu and was fortunate to have my parents taking care of me. They were so concerned that I wasn't eating and begged me to eat something . . . anything. The only thing I craved was rice pudding. My dad went on a mission, buying every type of rice pudding he could find in the tristate area, all in the hope that one of them would bring me back to health. It worked, and I'll always and forever be comforted by rice pudding. This version has an exotic spice twist from an infusion of cardamom, but feel free to use the traditional cinnamon or experiment with a spice of your choice.

1 cup uncooked jasmine rice

10 cardamom pods, seeds only (see tip), or 2 cinnamon sticks (optional)

½ cup sugar

¼ teaspoon kosher salt

4½ cups whole milk

2 teaspoons pure vanilla extract

¼ cup heavy cream

A dusting of cinnamon or whipped cream, for serving

1. In a medium saucepan, cook the rice until completely tender according to the package instructions.
2. Add the cardamom seeds (if using), sugar, salt, and 4 cups of the milk to the rice and simmer over low heat, stirring occasionally to keep the rice from sticking, until all the milk has been absorbed, about 40 minutes.
3. Stir in the remaining ½ cup milk, the vanilla, and the cream.
4. Transfer the pudding to a glass bowl, or for individual servings, into ceramic ramekins or glass dishes. Place a piece of plastic wrap flush on the surface of the pudding to keep a skin from forming. Refrigerate until ready to serve.

Serve with a dusting of cinnamon or whipped cream. I promise you'll feel cured!

* In order to extract the seeds from the cardamom pods, gently crush the pods with the bottom of a small sauté pan or a rolling pin or, if they're soft enough, peel them at the seam and pick the seeds out.

RANGER COOKIES

MAKES 36 COOKIES

This is my everything-but-the-kitchen-sink cookie! Chewy and chunky and crunchy and perfectly sweet, these ranger cookies are well balanced. They're great dunked into a big glass of milk or packed away for a picnic or used to refuel in the middle of a hike. Because they have cereal, cherries, and oats in them, I like to pretend they're a healthy dessert. Wink, wink.

Nonstick cooking spray
1 cup all-purpose flour
½ teaspoon baking soda
¼ teaspoon baking powder
¼ teaspoon kosher salt
½ cup vegetable shortening
½ cup granulated sugar
½ cup packed light brown sugar
2 large eggs
½ teaspoon pure vanilla extract
1 cup quick-cooking oats
1 cup Special K cereal
1 cup semisweet chocolate chips
½ cup sweetened coconut flakes
½ cup dried cherries, chopped

PREP: CHOP THE DRIED CHERRIES

1. Preheat the oven to 350°F. Grease three baking sheets with nonstick cooking spray.
2. Sift the flour, baking soda, baking powder, and salt into a large bowl.
3. In the bowl of a stand mixer fitted with the paddle attachment, or in a large bowl using a hand mixer, beat the shortening, sugars, eggs, and vanilla until fluffy.
4. Set the mixer on low speed and gradually add the sifted dry ingredients, mixing until the dough comes together.
5. Turn off the machine. Use a wooden spoon to mix in the oats, cereal, chocolate chips, coconut flakes, and dried cherries until just incorporated. This cookie dough is looser than most, so refrigerate it for about 1 hour before baking to prevent the dough from spreading too much.

6. Drop the dough by rounded tablespoons 2 inches apart on the prepared baking sheets.

7. Bake until golden brown, around 15 minutes. After the first 7 or 8 minutes, rotate the baking sheets to ensure even baking.

8. Let the cookies cool on the baking sheets for about 1 minute, then transfer to a wire rack to cool completely.

*** Cooling any cookies on the baking sheet for 1 to 2 minutes after removing them from the oven makes for a moister cookie, as the steam generated between the cookie and the sheet is trapped in the cookie. For a firmer, more crumbly texture, immediately transfer cookies to a rack. The increased airflow allows them to dry more quickly.**

CHOCOLATE TRUFFLES

MAKES 36 TRUFFLES

Chocolate is one of my desert island ingredients, and this recipe ticks all the dessert boxes. Easy? Check. Impressive? Check. Can be prepared ahead of time? Check. Can lick the bowl? Double check!

1 cup heavy cream

8 ounces dark or semisweet chocolate, chopped

Pinch of sea salt

1 cup unsweetened cocoa powder

1. Bring the heavy cream to a simmer in a small stainless-steel or other nonreactive saucepan. Turn off the heat, add the chocolate, and stir until it's fully melted.
2. Transfer the hot mixture to a large bowl. Use a whisk to whip the mixture, ensuring the chocolate and cream are fully combined.
3. Refrigerate the mixture until firm, about 30 minutes.
4. Put the cocoa powder in a bowl or shallow baking dish and have it nearby. Using a 1-tablespoon-size ice cream scoop, distribute even scoops of the mixture onto a baking sheet. If you don't have the proper scoop, use a rounded tablespoon measure to portion.
5. Use your clean hands to roll each ball as perfectly even and round as possible. But try not to handle the chocolate for too long, as the heat of your hands will melt it.
6. Drop each truffle into the cocoa and roll it around, coating it in the powder. Use a spoon or your fingers to remove the truffle from the powder and transfer to a container large enough to hold one or two batches. Choose a container that allows you to layer the truffles, using waxed paper between layers.
7. Refrigerate the truffles until ready to serve.

* Remember, it's fun for everyone to know that you just whipped up a batch of truffles, so it's fine if they're a little rustic in appearance! They'll taste just as decadent.

PEANUT BUTTER BLONDIES

MAKES 12 SQUARES

As a chocolate lover, I could easily have filled this chapter with chocolate-based recipes, but I had to restrain myself. So instead of my brownie recipe, here's a peanut butter blondie recipe that I adore. But don't worry—I still manage to sneak chocolate in there, by drizzling them with chocolate sauce, eating them with chocolate milk, or even gluing two together into a sandwich with chocolate mousse filling (see page 265).

Nonstick cooking spray

2½ cups all-purpose flour

½ teaspoon baking soda

½ teaspoon kosher salt

1 cup (2 sticks) unsalted butter, at room temperature

¾ cup sugar

2 large eggs

1 (10-ounce) package peanut butter chips

1. Preheat the oven to 350°F and make sure the oven rack is in the center position. Grease a 9 × 13-inch baking pan with nonstick cooking spray.
2. Combine the flour, baking soda, and salt in a medium bowl. Use a fork or whisk to combine.
3. In the bowl of a stand mixer fitted with the paddle attachment, or in a large bowl using a hand mixer (or even in a food processor), cream the butter and sugar until pale yellow and fluffy. Add the eggs and mix to incorporate fully.
4. With the mixer running on low, gradually add the dry ingredients, letting each addition be fully incorporated before you add more.
5. Turn off the machine and use a wooden spoon or rubber spatula to scrape down the sides of the bowl. Mix once or twice more to fully incorporate all the flour.
6. Remove the bowl from the mixer. Add the peanut butter chips and use a spoon or spatula to mix just until the chips have been distributed throughout the batter.

7. Transfer the batter to the prepared baking pan and use the spoon or spatula to push it into the corners, making a smooth, even layer.

8. Bake until a toothpick or skewer inserted into the center comes out clean and the blondies are golden, 18 to 20 minutes. Allow to cool before cutting into squares.

MENUS

Sunday Supper

Jersey Sunday Meatballs, 149
Marinara Sauce, 35
Mixed Marinated Olives, 70
Caesar Salad with Homemade Butter Croutons, 89
Broccolini with Lemon and Rosemary, 194

Easter Dinner

Marinated Artichokes, 209
Basic Risotto, 3
Salmon with Peas, Pearl Onions, and Mint, 130
Angel Food Cake, 253

Mother's Day Brunch

Spinach, Potato, and Ricotta Egg White Frittata, 119
Buttermilk Biscuits, 218
Herb Pesto, 36
Oven-Roasted Tomatoes, 12
Lobster Salad, 110
Cocoa Carrot Cake with Cream Cheese Icing, 273

•Summer Soiree

Gazpacho, 66

Grilled Zucchini and Tomato Panzanella Salad, 107

Grilled Steak with Herb Butter, 135

Summer Berry Fruit Crumble, 261

•Backyard BBQ

Pulled Pork Sandwiches, 159

No-Nonsense Coleslaw, 193

Giardiniera, 190

Orzo Pasta Salad, 197

Peanut Butter Blondies, 282

Ranger Cookies, 278

•Fall Harvest Celebration/Thanksgiving

Butternut Squash Soup, 68

All-Around Mustard Sauce, 47

Your favorite roast turkey

Cornbread and Challah Stuffing, 186

Green Beans with Toasted Almonds, 185

Yogurt Panna Cotta with Dried Cranberry and Grape Compote, 267

•Winter Warm-Up

Potato-Kale Soup, 169

Beef Short Ribs, 171

Root Vegetable Puree, 200

Shallot Confit, 16

Rice Pudding Is the Cure!, 276

• Easy French

Easy Coq au Vin, 239

Kale and Farro Salad with Aged Goat Cheese, 94

Corn Soufflé, 223

Coconut Macaroons, 262

• Romantic Dinner

Duck Breast with
Pine Nut Relish, 247

Blanched haricot verts, 9,
with Mustard Vinaigrette, 24

Crispy Spaetzle with
Roasted Sunchokes, 235

Chocolate Truffles, 280

• Happy New Year!

French Onion Soup, 8

Crabmeat Crostini, 76

Shrimp Cocktail with
Homemade Sauce, 72

Mediterranean Potato Salad, 198

Herb-Stuffed Whole Fish, 241

Impressive Dark Chocolate
Mousse, 265

ACKNOWLEDGMENTS

The task of letting the people in my life know how grateful I am for them seems almost greater than writing this book. I have never been filled with more gratitude than I am today. I hope these words will be able to convey how truly thankful I am.

First and foremost, I would like to thank Kari Stuart—without you, this book would never have happened. Thank you for believing in me and this idea for so long and never giving up on it. I appreciate your support and guidance.

To Carrie King, you're the backbone of this book. You're the most patient, smart, funny, talented, and wonderful writer, cook, and friend. Thank you for being so flexible and doing whatever it took to get this done. I've learned so much from you and shared so many wonderful moments during this project, and I can't wait to do it again!

To Cassie Jones and all of the amazing publishing people at William Morrow, who helped make this book a reality, including Kara Zauberman, Liate Stehlik, Lynn Grady, Andy Dodds, Tavia Kowalchuk, Rachel Meyers, Lorie Pagnozzi, and Anna Brower.

To the dream team of food photography and styling:

To David Malosh—without your vision, talent, and kindness, I would have never been able to create the gorgeous images that lie on these pages. You helped bring out the best in me and never let me doubt my imagination. The words *thank you* will never be enough.

To Barrett Washburne—you, my friend, are a rock star! Not only did you help me put the dream team together, you were the conductor of the symphony. You have such skill as a food stylist, and I'm so lucky to have had you on this project. You're a brilliant chef and artist. I knew this book was going to be a success when after the first week of shooting you said, "Amanda, your cookbook is making me fat!" Ah, victory!

To Nico Sherman—thank you for your wonderful work assisting in the kitchen, and most of all for making me laugh! The environment that surrounds me while I'm working always influences the outcome, and you brought such joy to the kitchen and made so many wonderful memories.

To Kendall Mills—thank you for being an expert part of the team and having such a great eye.

Thank you to the whole team at Columbia Products Studio, especially Adrien and Billy, for keeping us nourished and healthy and welcoming us into your home.

To Natalie Kendall, for the many hours you spent testing recipes and deciphering my handwriting. I'm so grateful for your eagerness to take on such a big task.

To my mom—thanks, Momma, for always being superproud of my accomplishments, whether they were big or small. Maybe now that I have a cookbook you'll let me come mess up your kitchen!

To Jason and Justin—thank you for being my big brothers and always looking out for me. I know I always tried to be the tough one, but I wouldn't have been this strong without you guys.

To Karla and Oksana—for being patient and loving with my brothers and becoming a part of our family.

To Lizzie and Megan—you're such amazing young women, and you inspire me to be my best always. Thank you for making me feel like the coolest aunt on the planet.

To Rafael—thank you, thank you for being the best support system a girl could ever ask for. Your patience and positivity know no bounds. I'm so lucky to have you in my life. I love you.

To all the chefs who have taught me and influenced my career—I would be nothing without you. In particular, Diane Forley, who shaped me into the chef I am today.

To all my *Chopped* crew—thank you, Aaron, Alex, Chris, Geoffrey, Marcus, Maneet, Marc, Scott, Ted, and the rest of the team. You're my extended family, and I've learned so much from all of you.

Last but not least, to my friends, who always knew I could do it even when I didn't. Thank you a million times over, Pam, David, Ariane, John, Gregor, Laura, Todd, Amy and Amy, Nate, Seamus, Lauren, Myra, Austin, Tiffany, Vera, Victoria, and many more.

INDEX

NOTE: Page references in italics refer to photos of recipes.

A

B

C

D

E

I

J

K

L

M

N

O

S

T

V

W

Y

Z